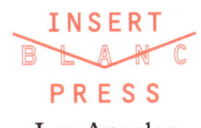

INSERT
BLANC
PRESS
Los Angeles

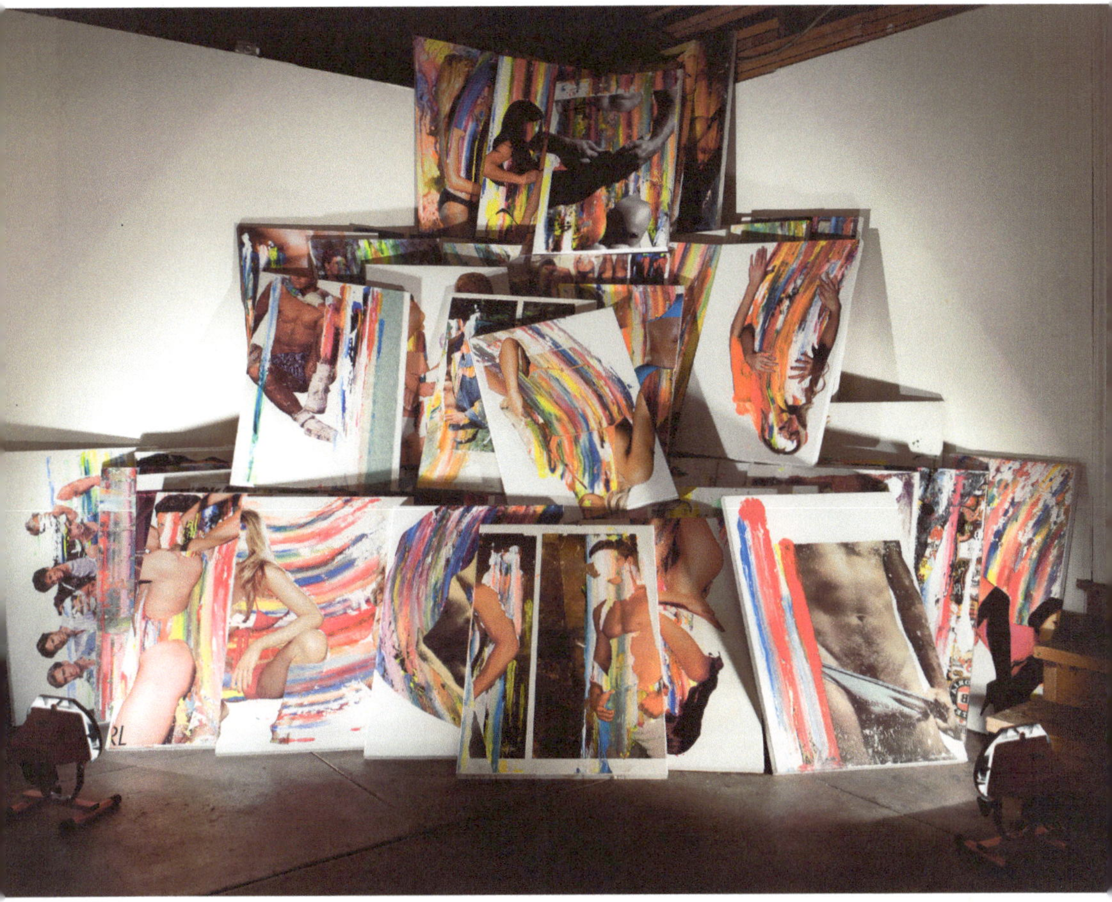

REFUSE PRIZE
© Greg Curtis Ben White
Insert Blanc Press 2015
ISBN: 978-0-9961696-1-5

Photography by Michael Underwood

This work was previously exhibited at Elephant Art Space
and The Phoebe Conley Gallery at CSU Fresno.

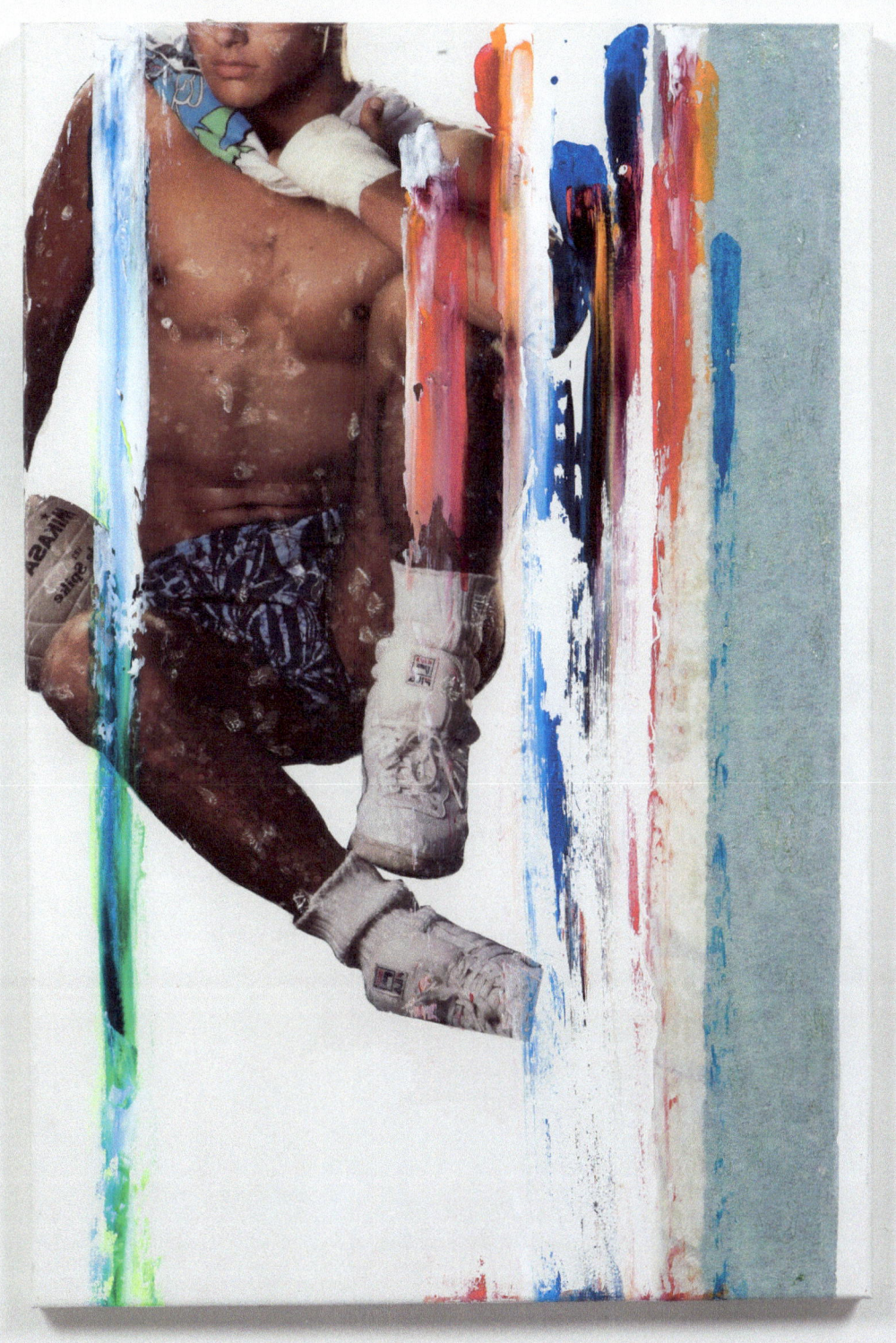

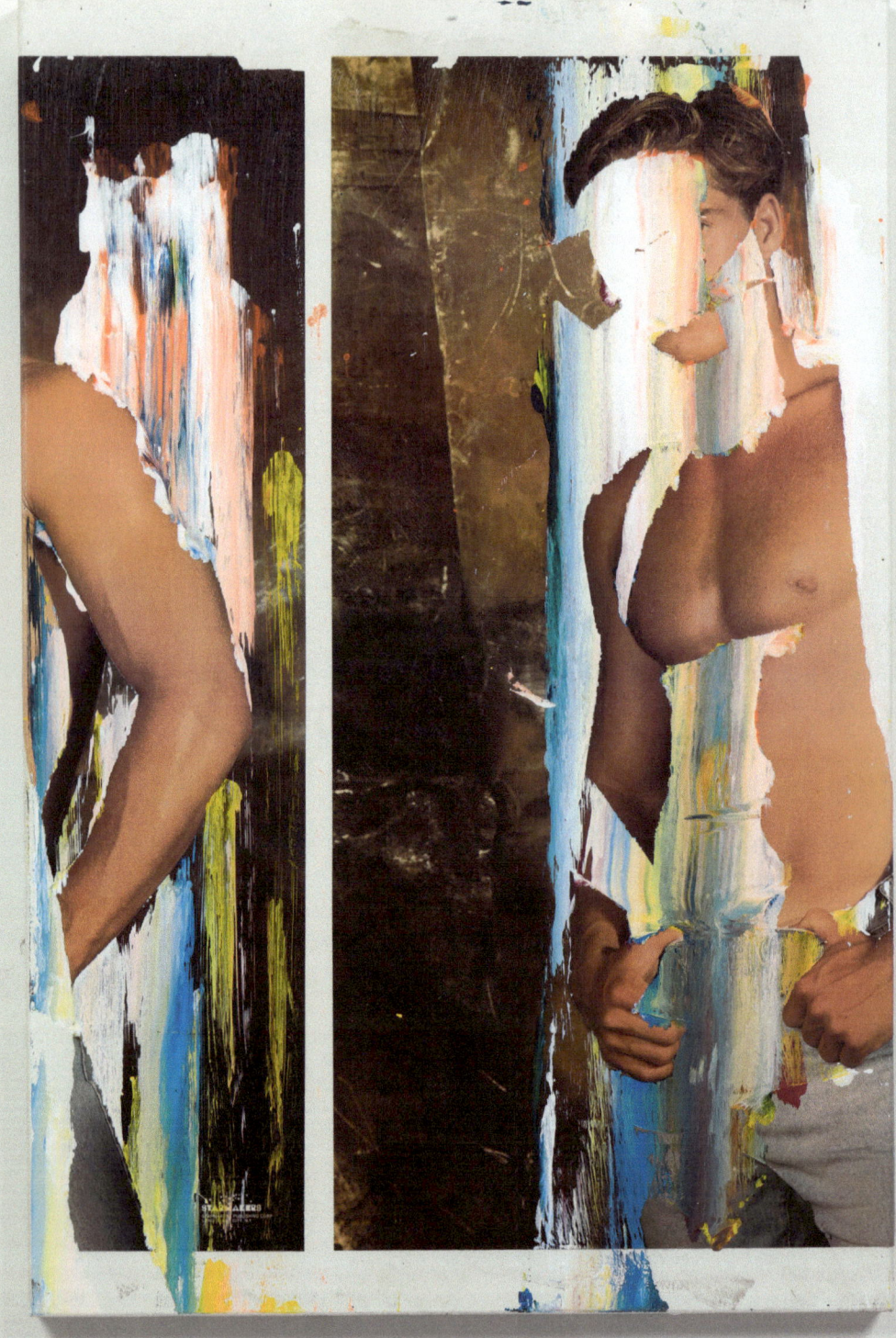

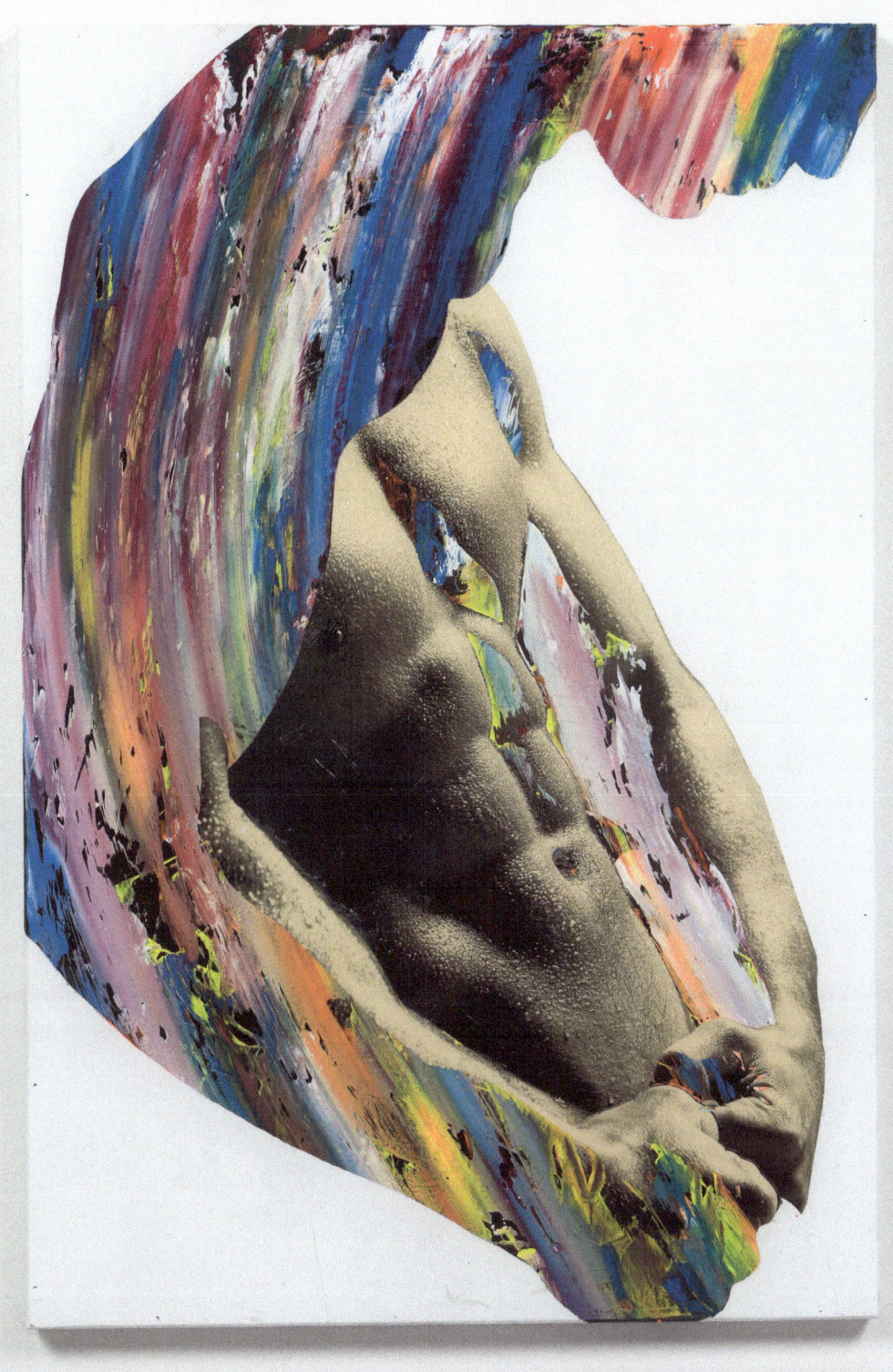

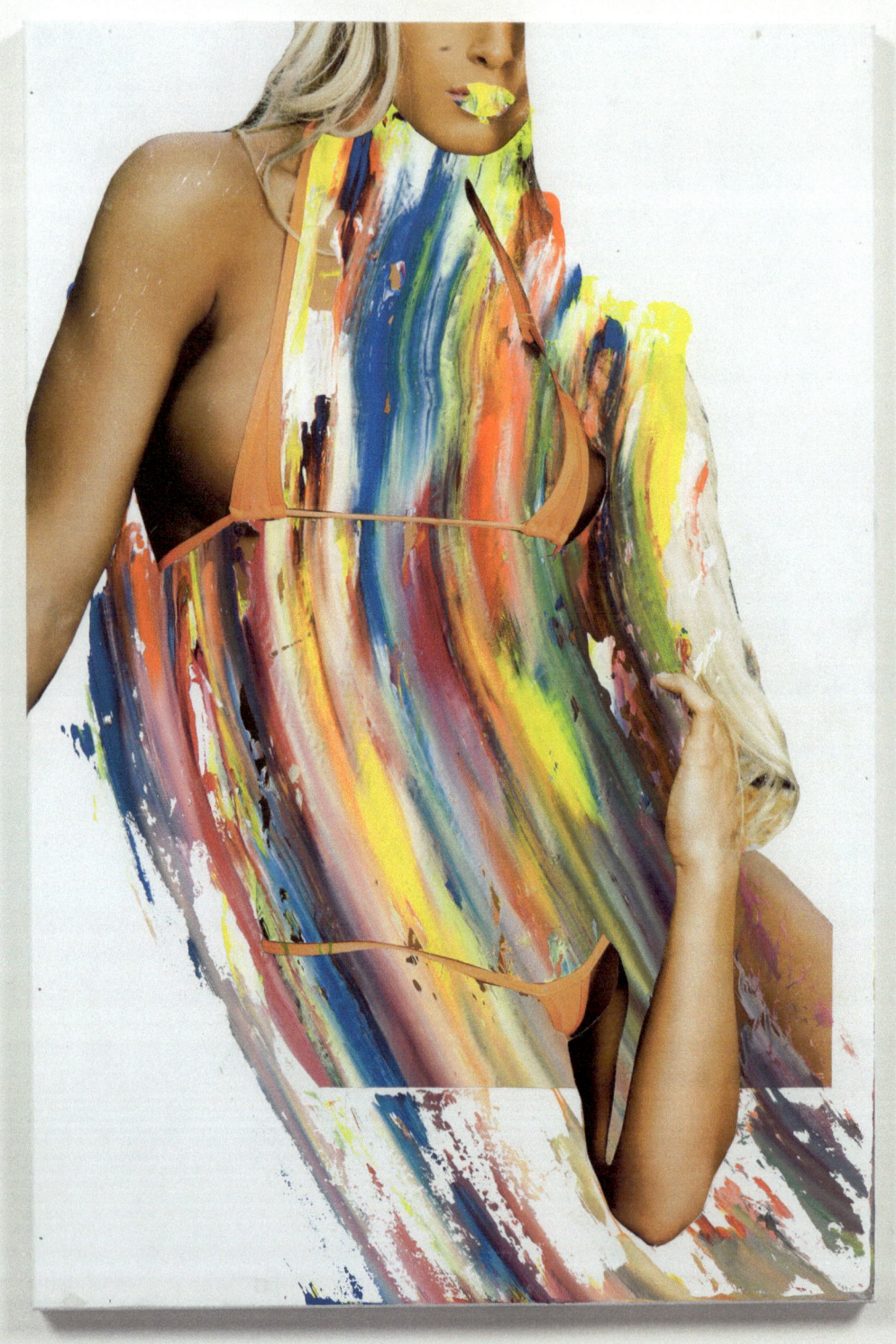

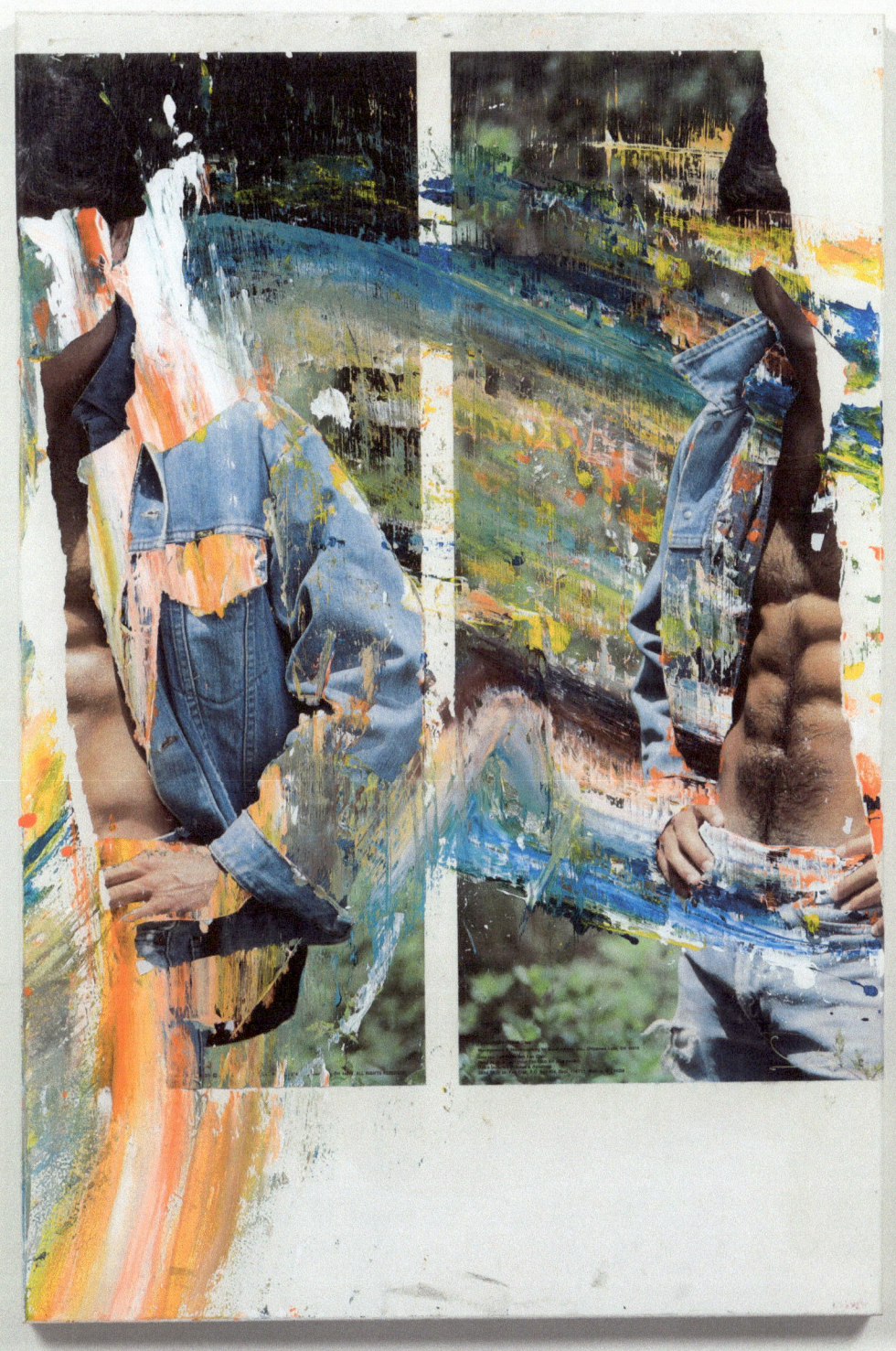

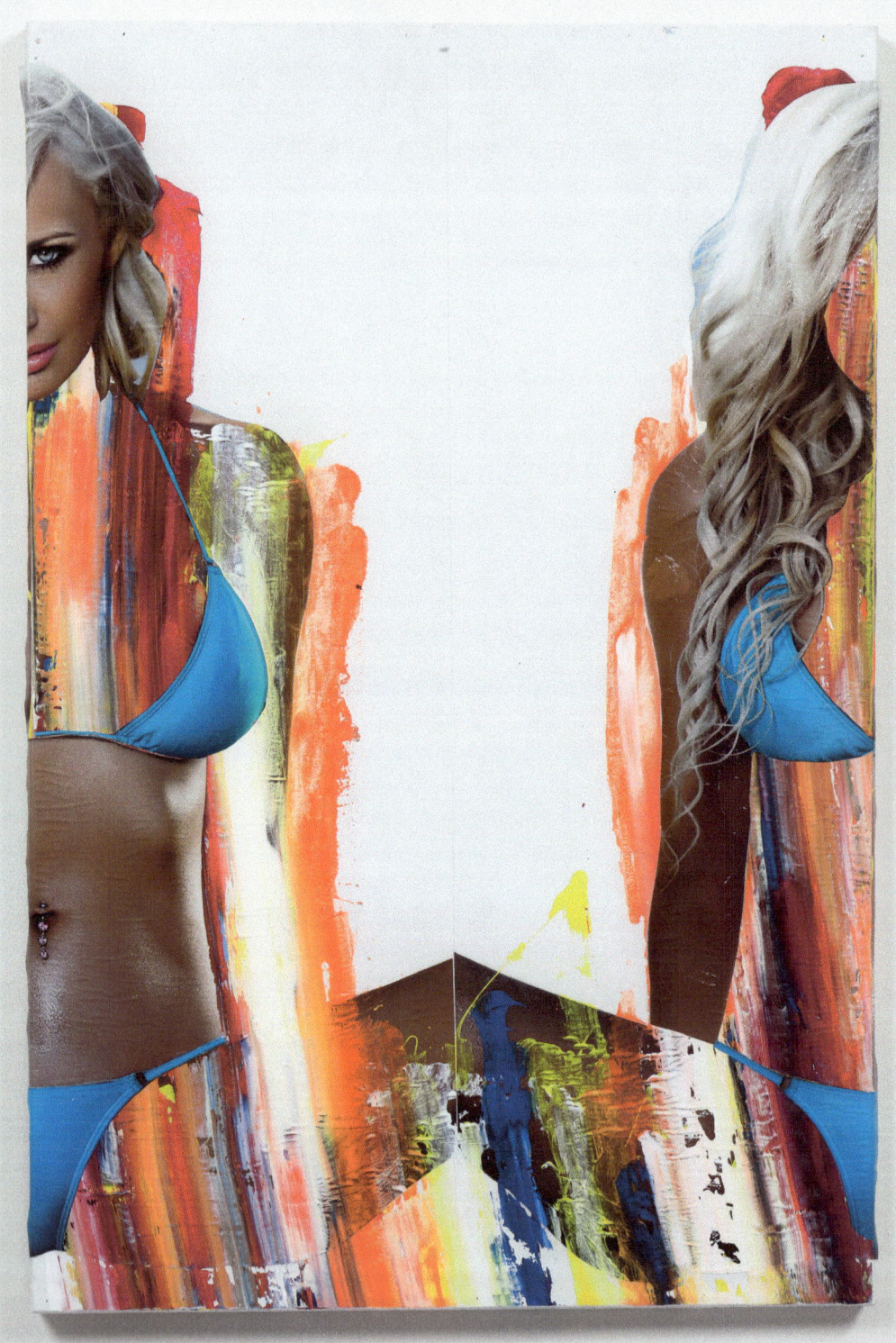

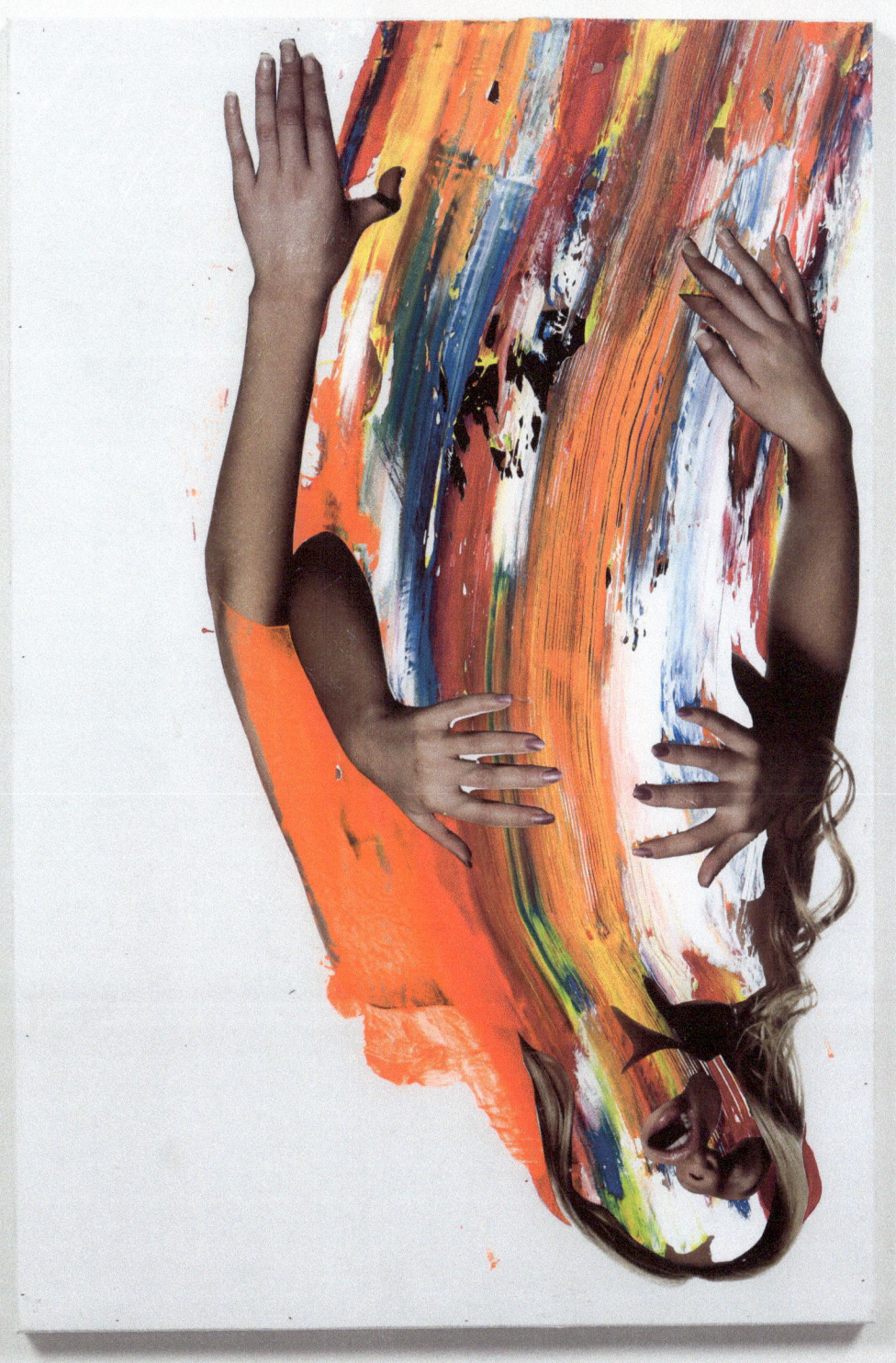

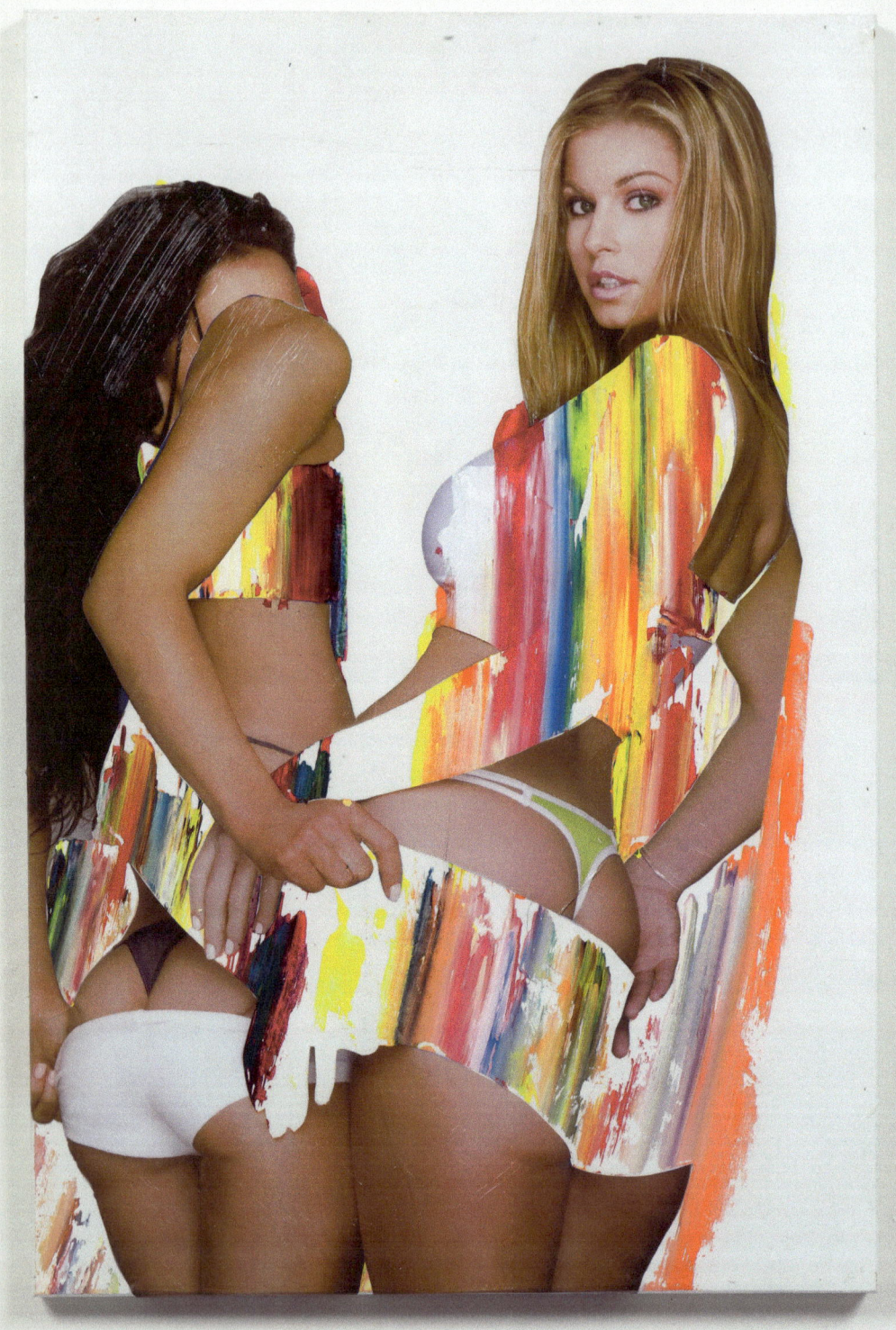

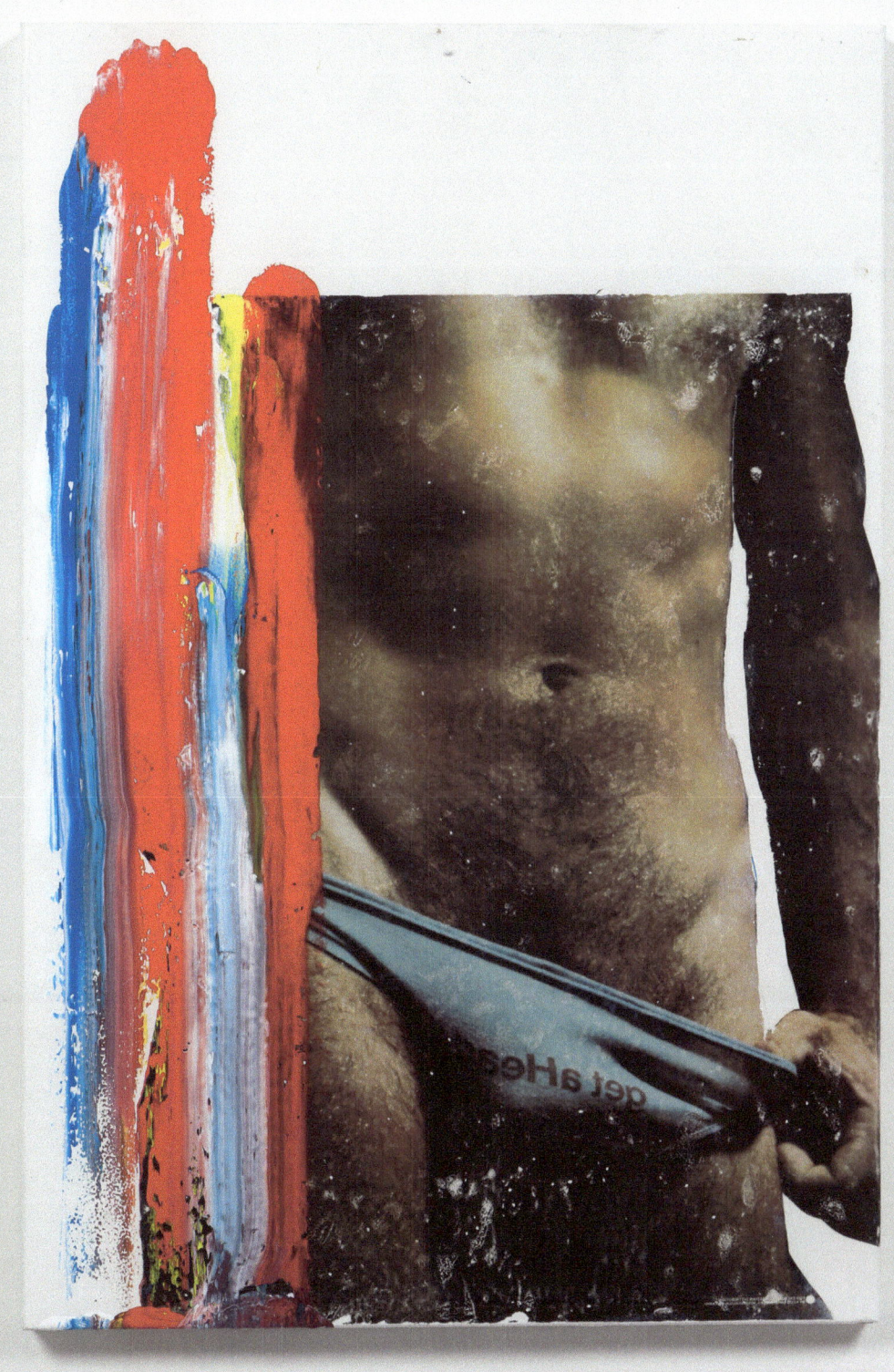

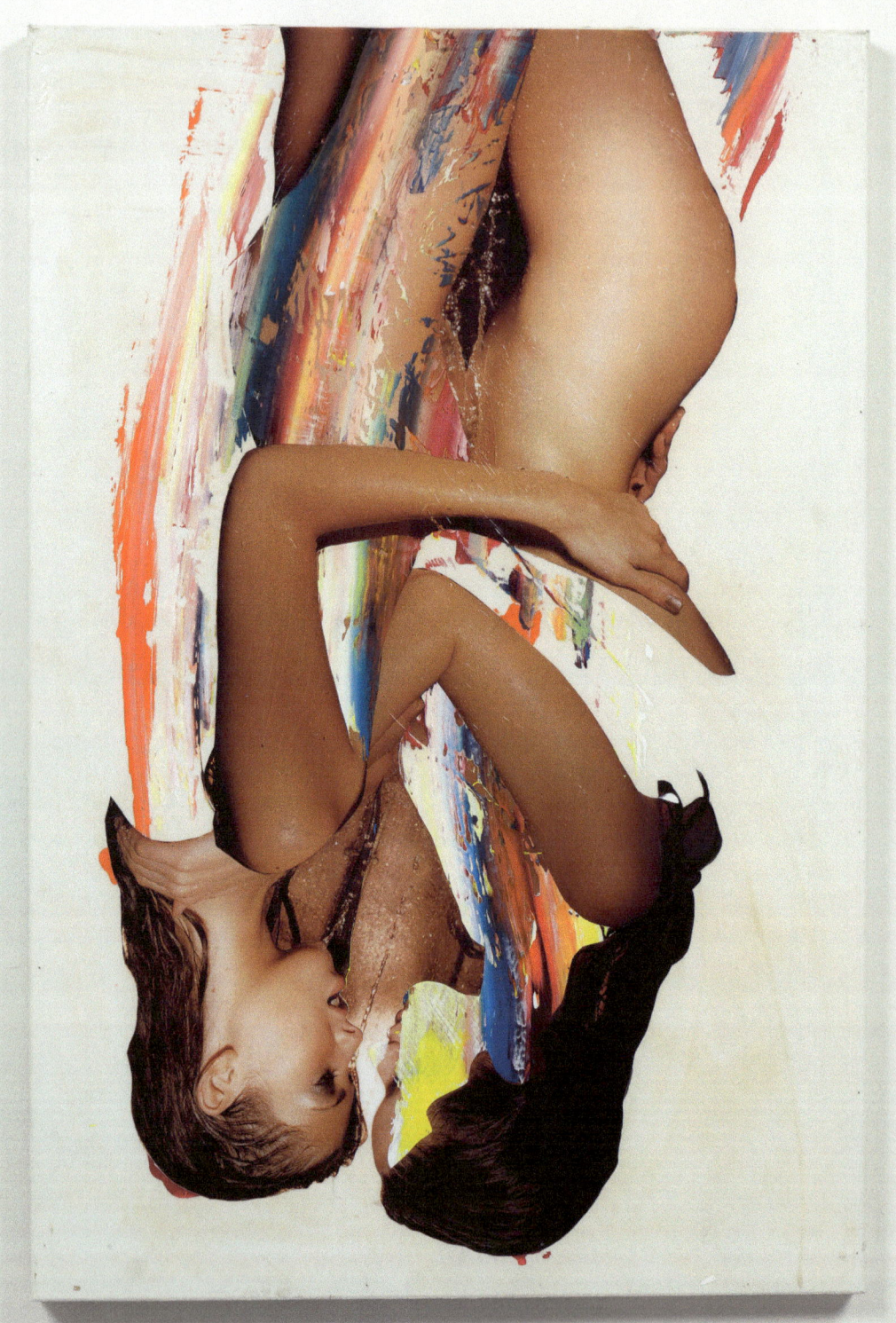

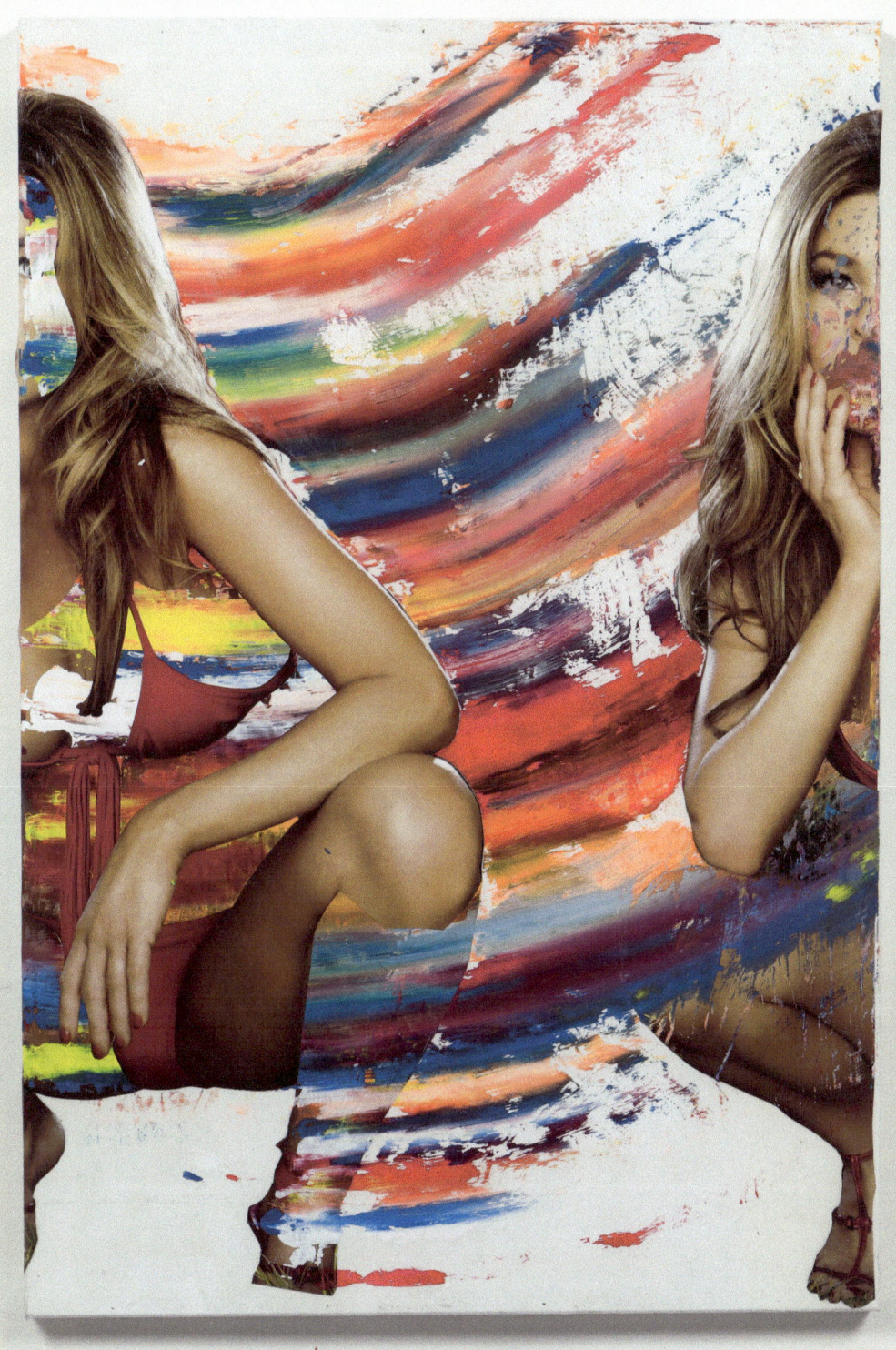

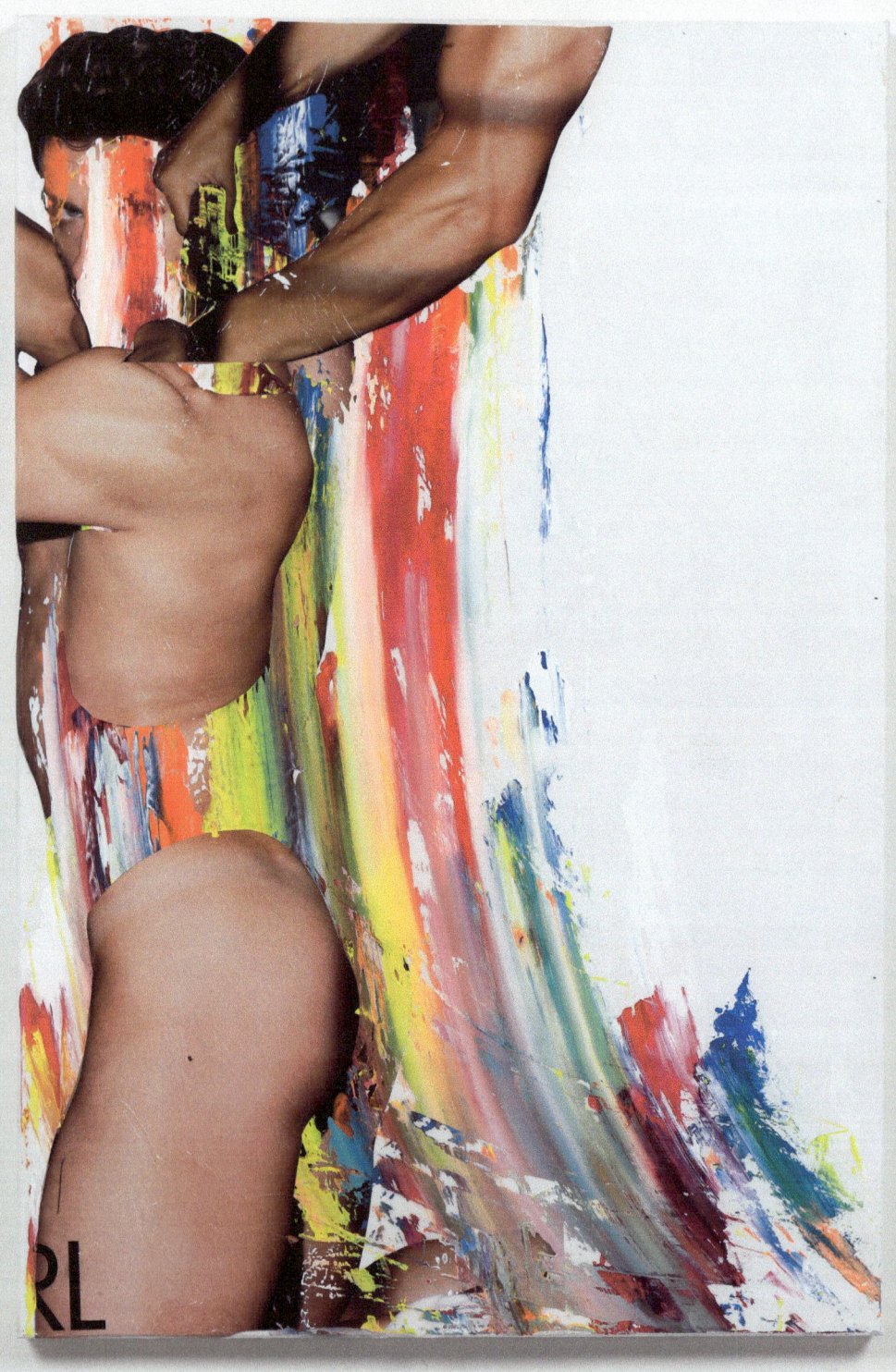

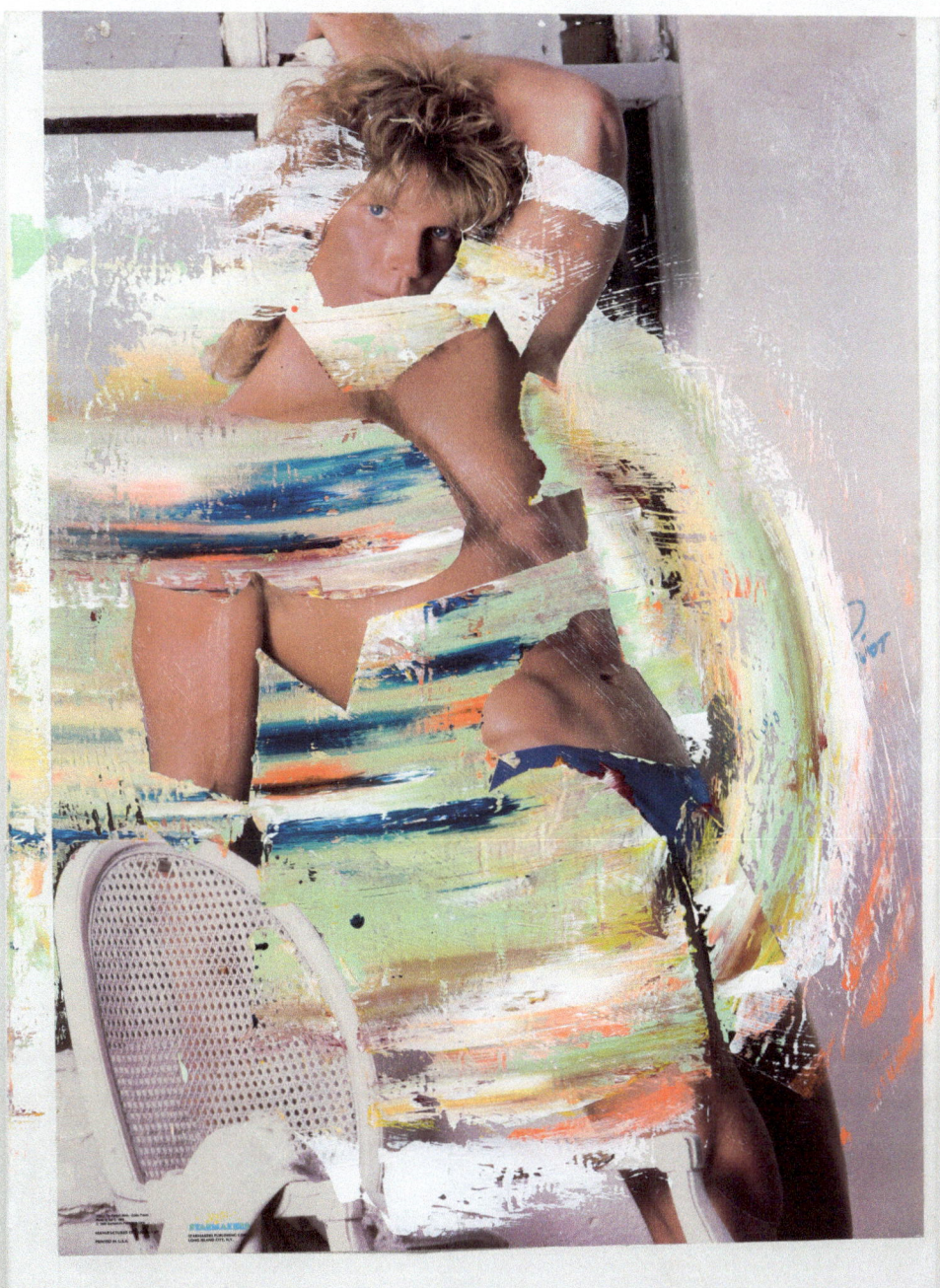

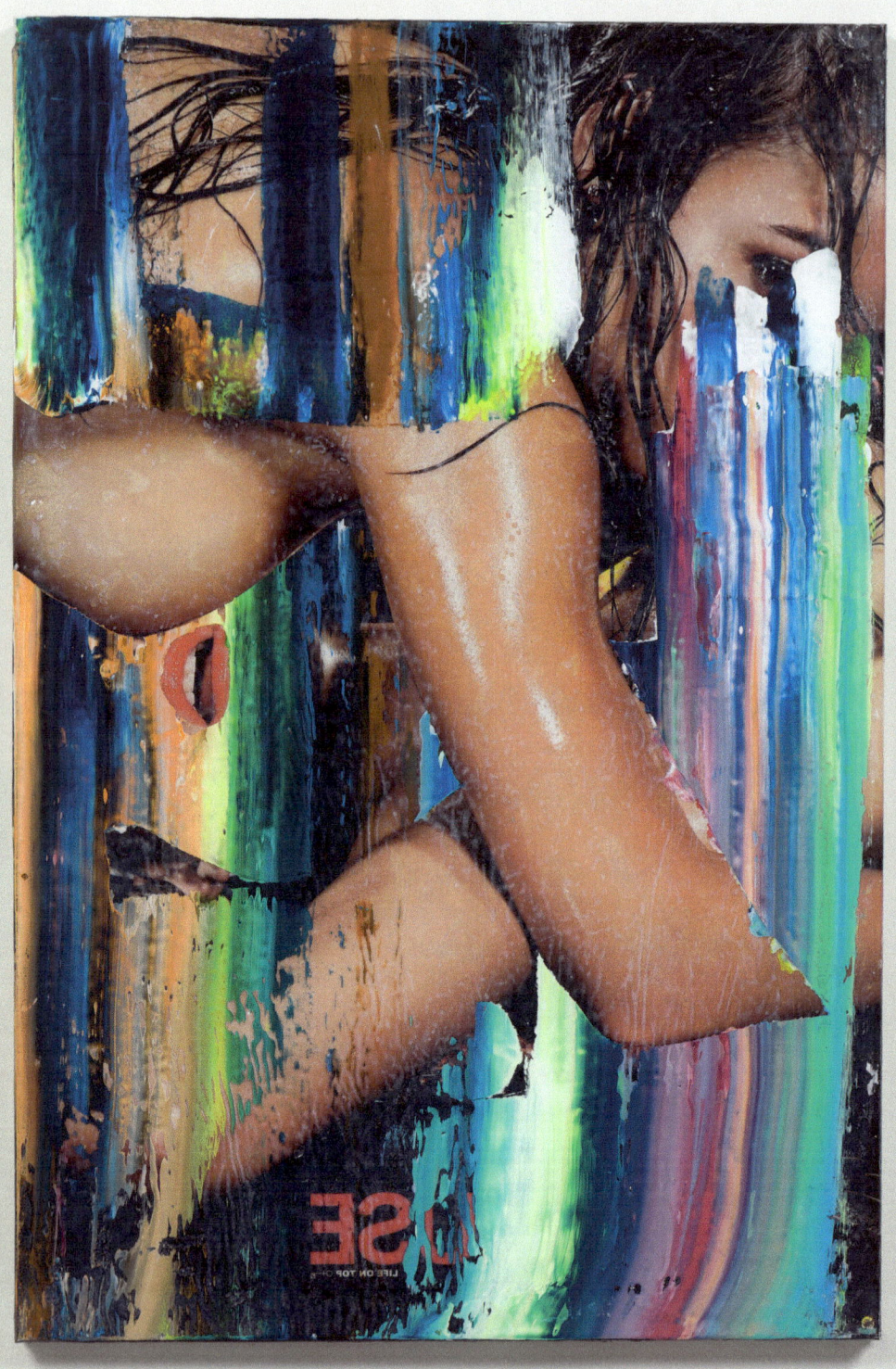

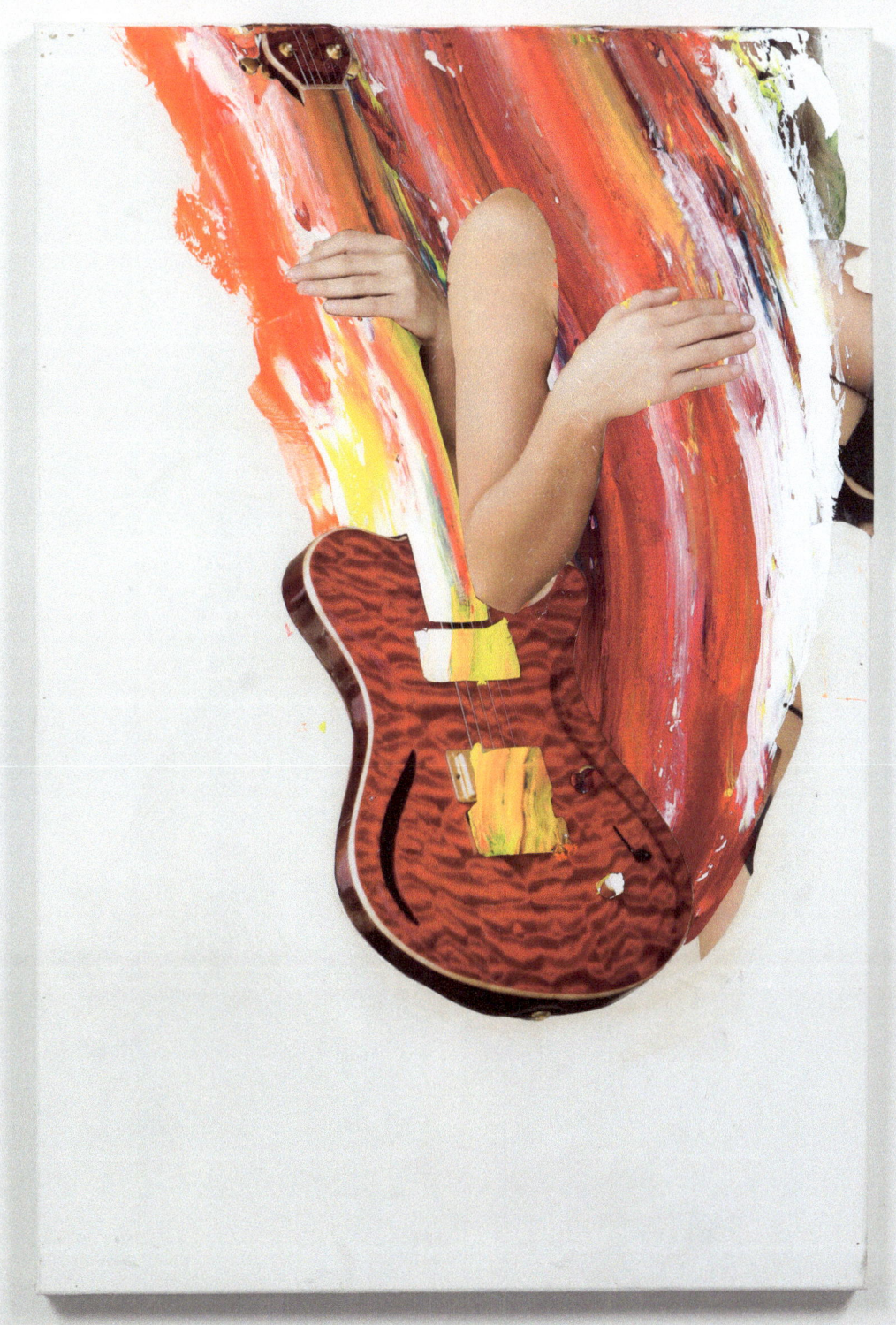

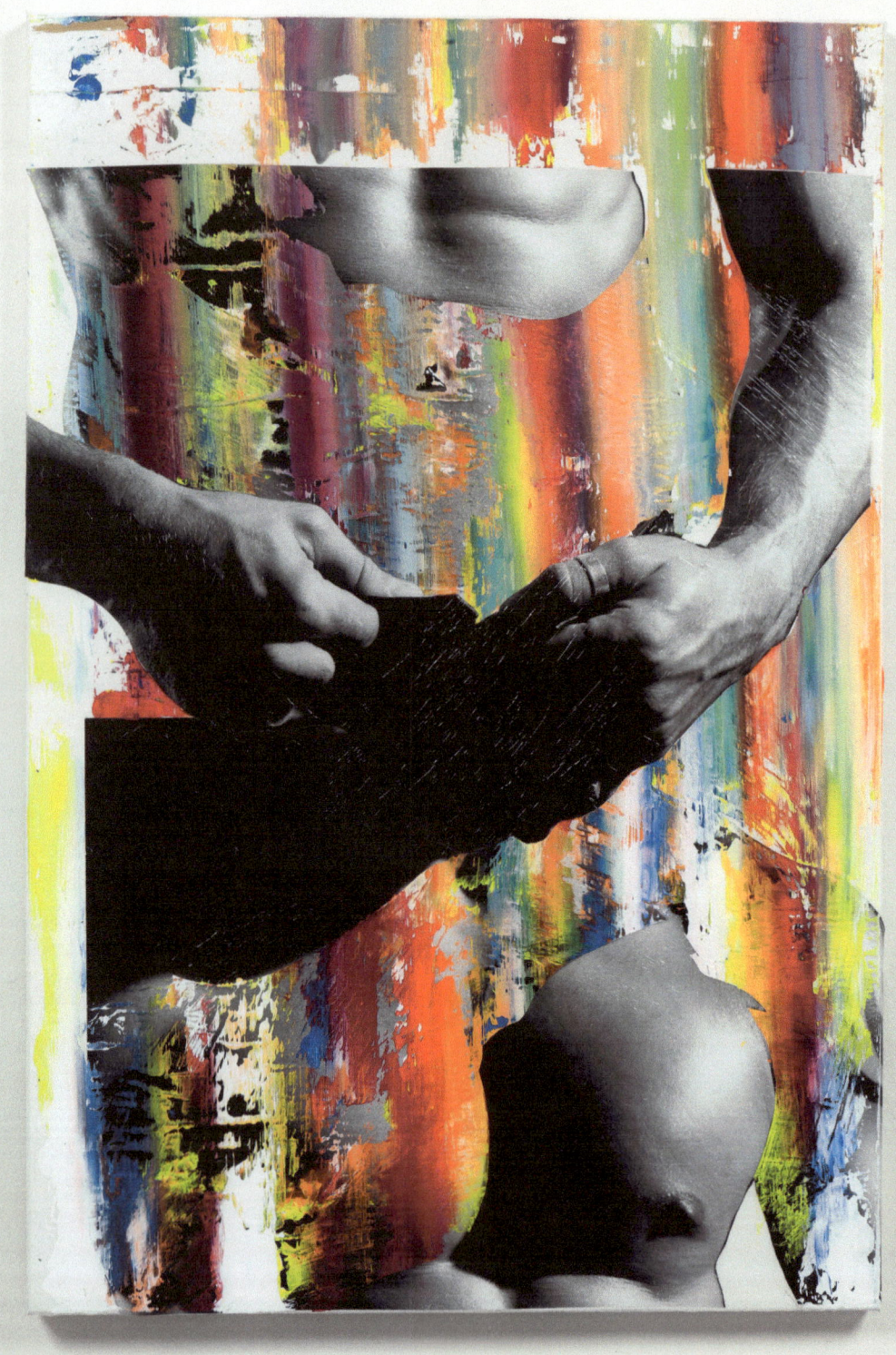

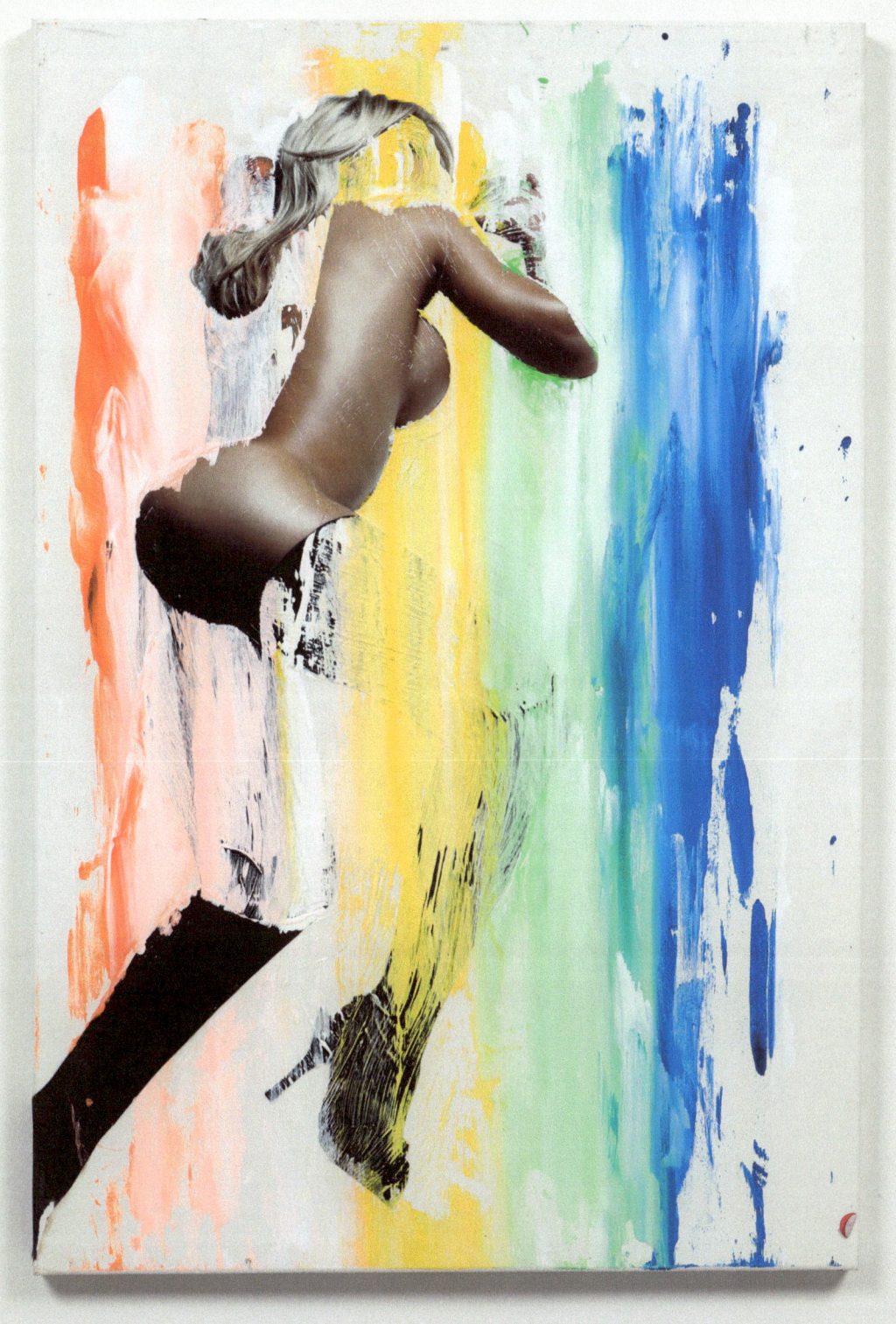

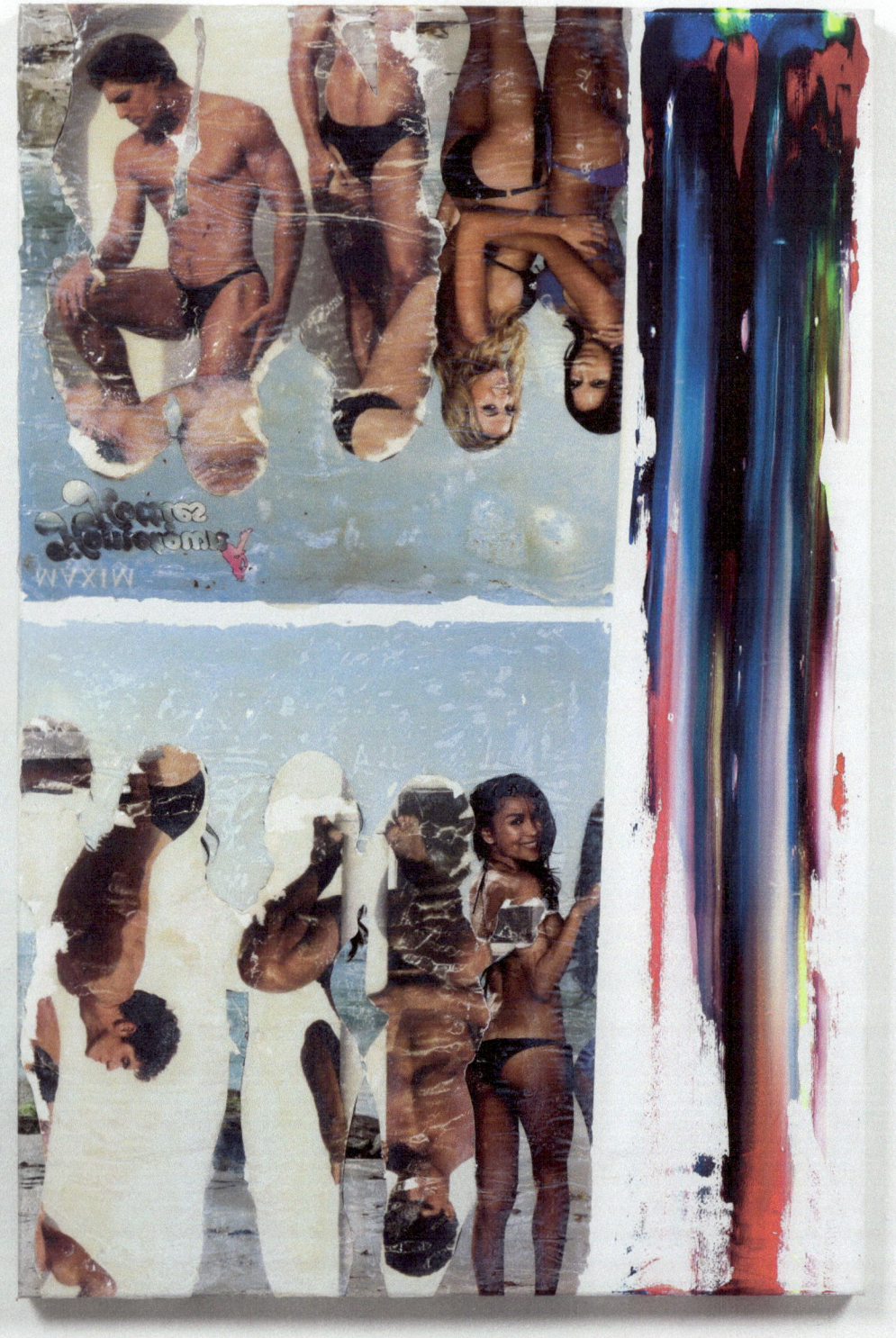

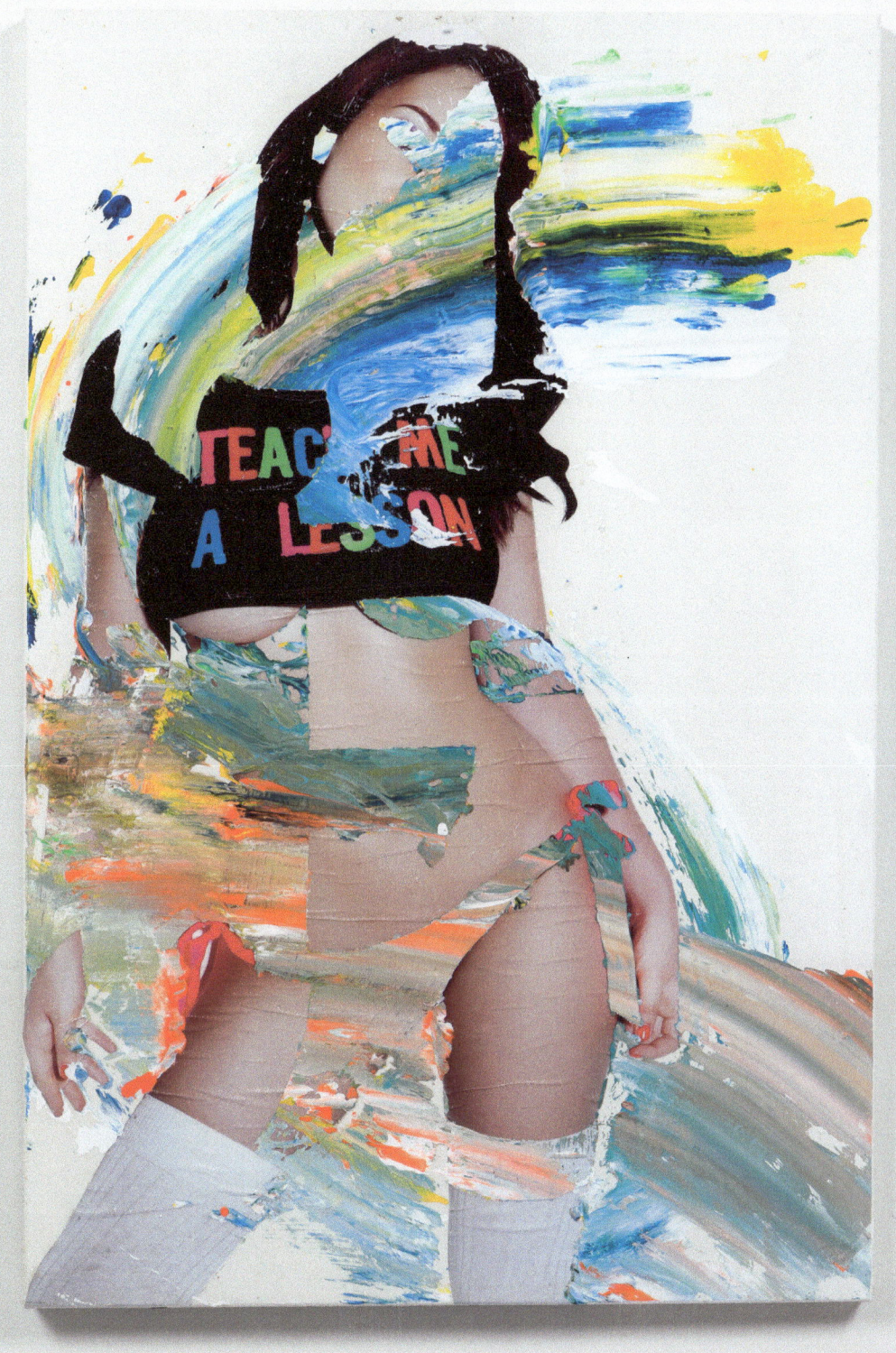

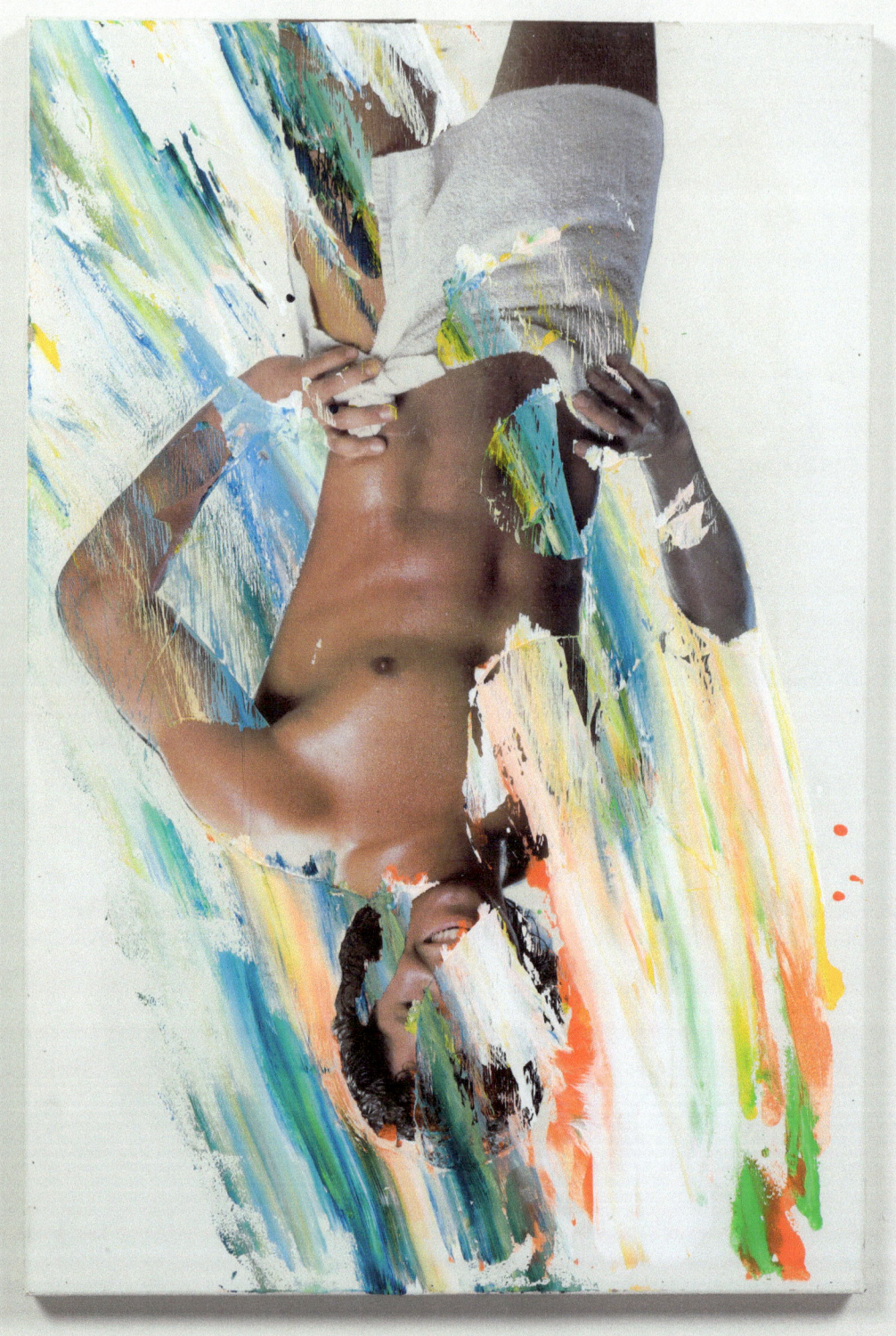

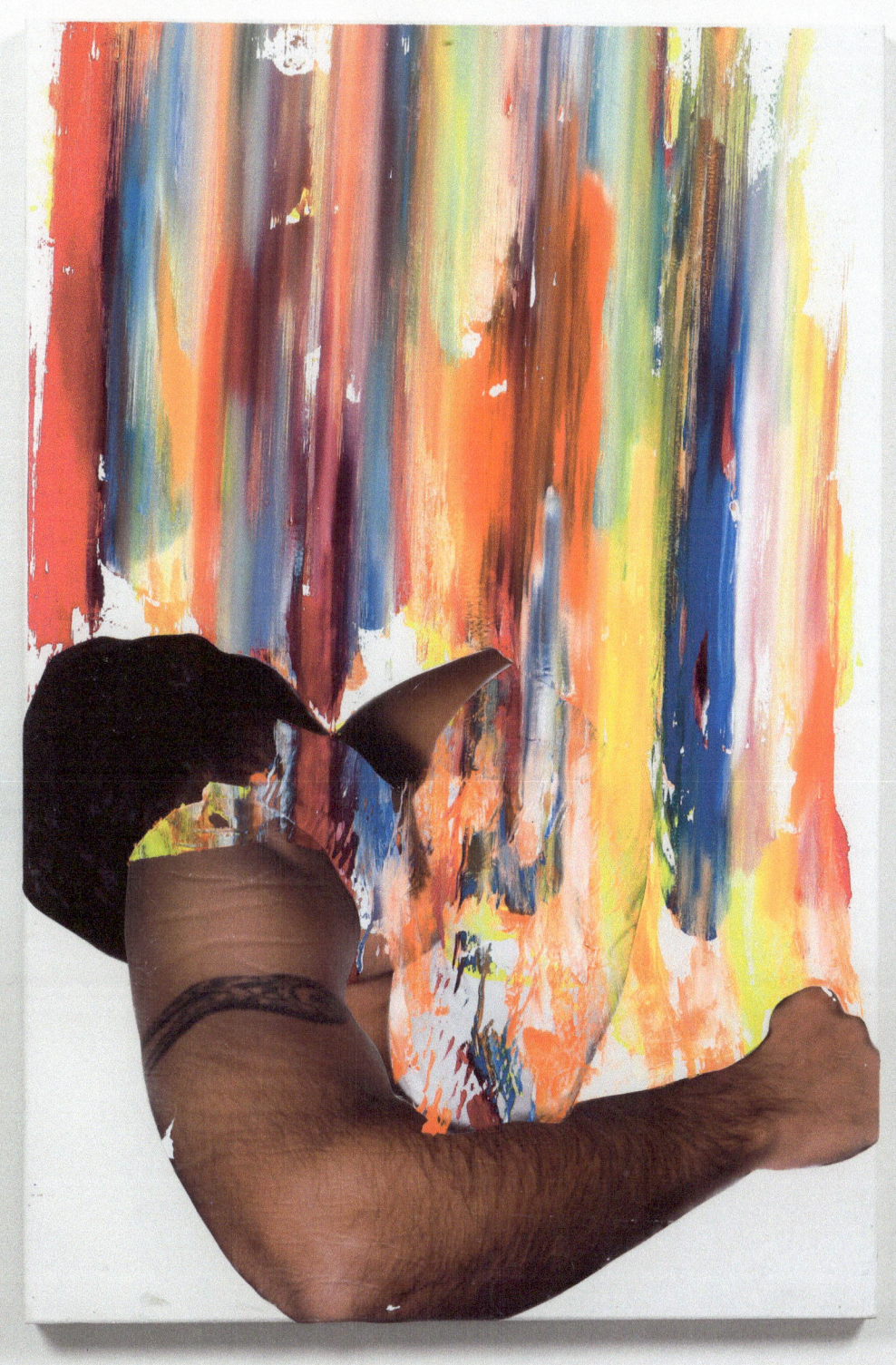

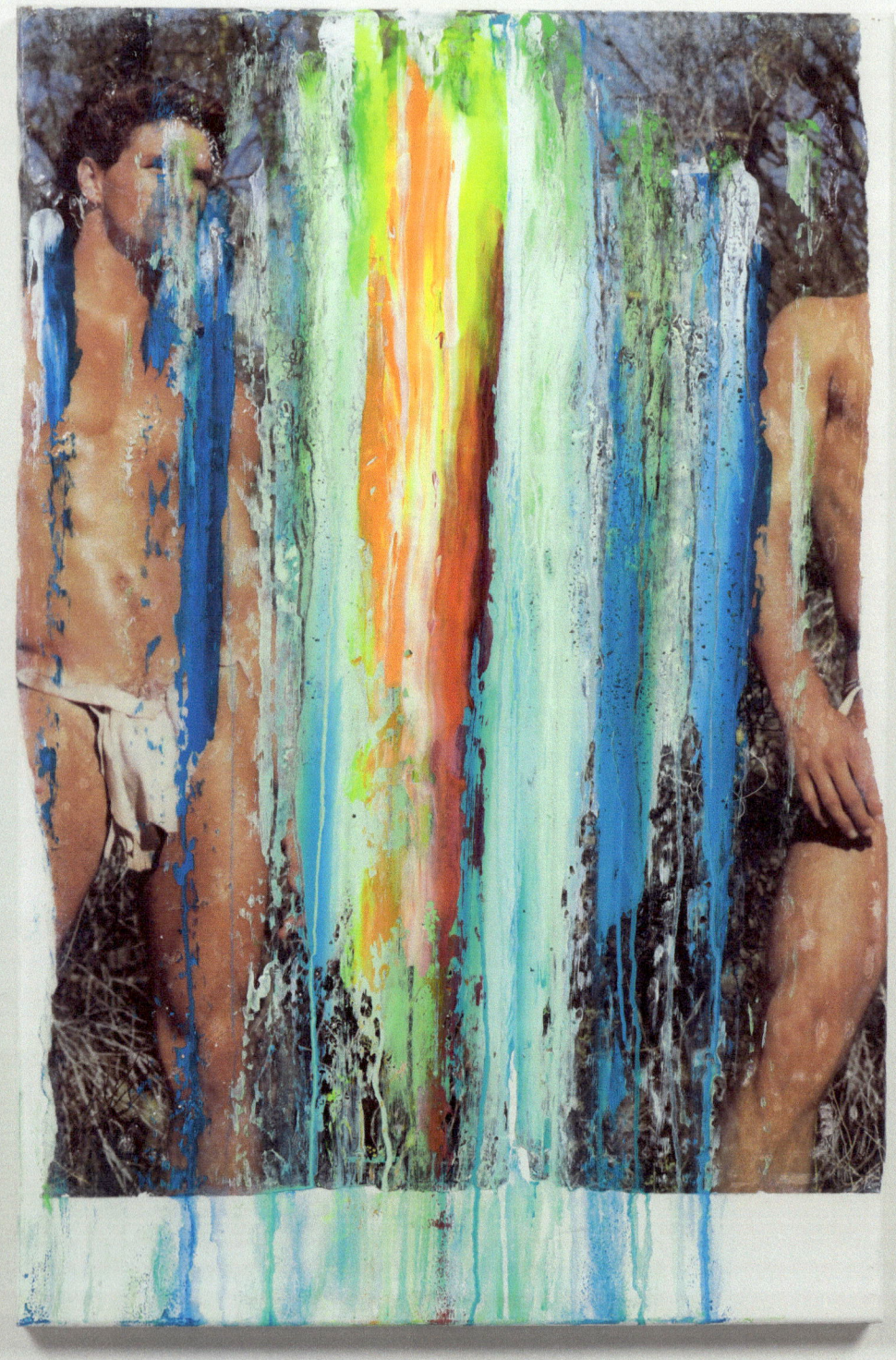

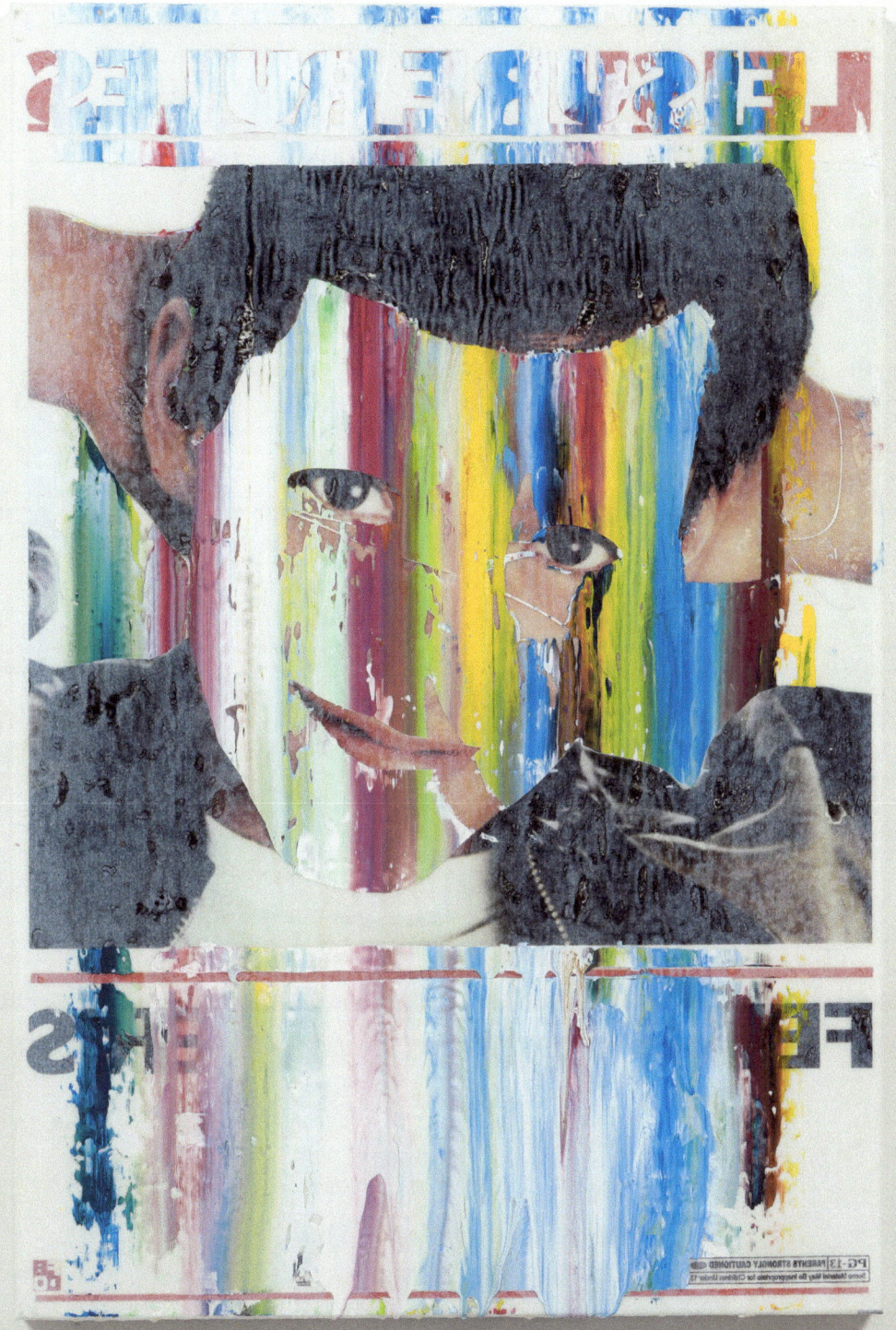

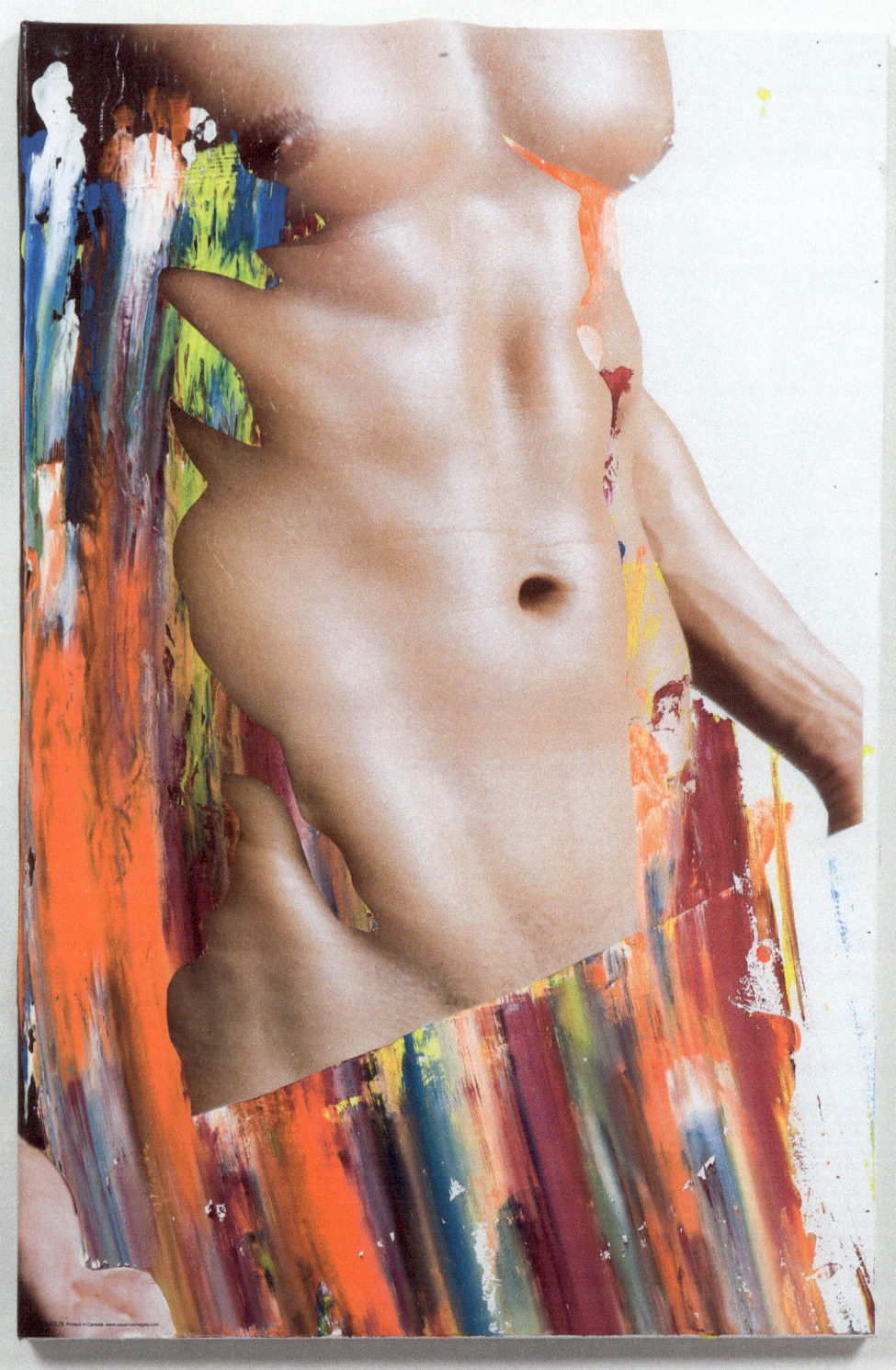

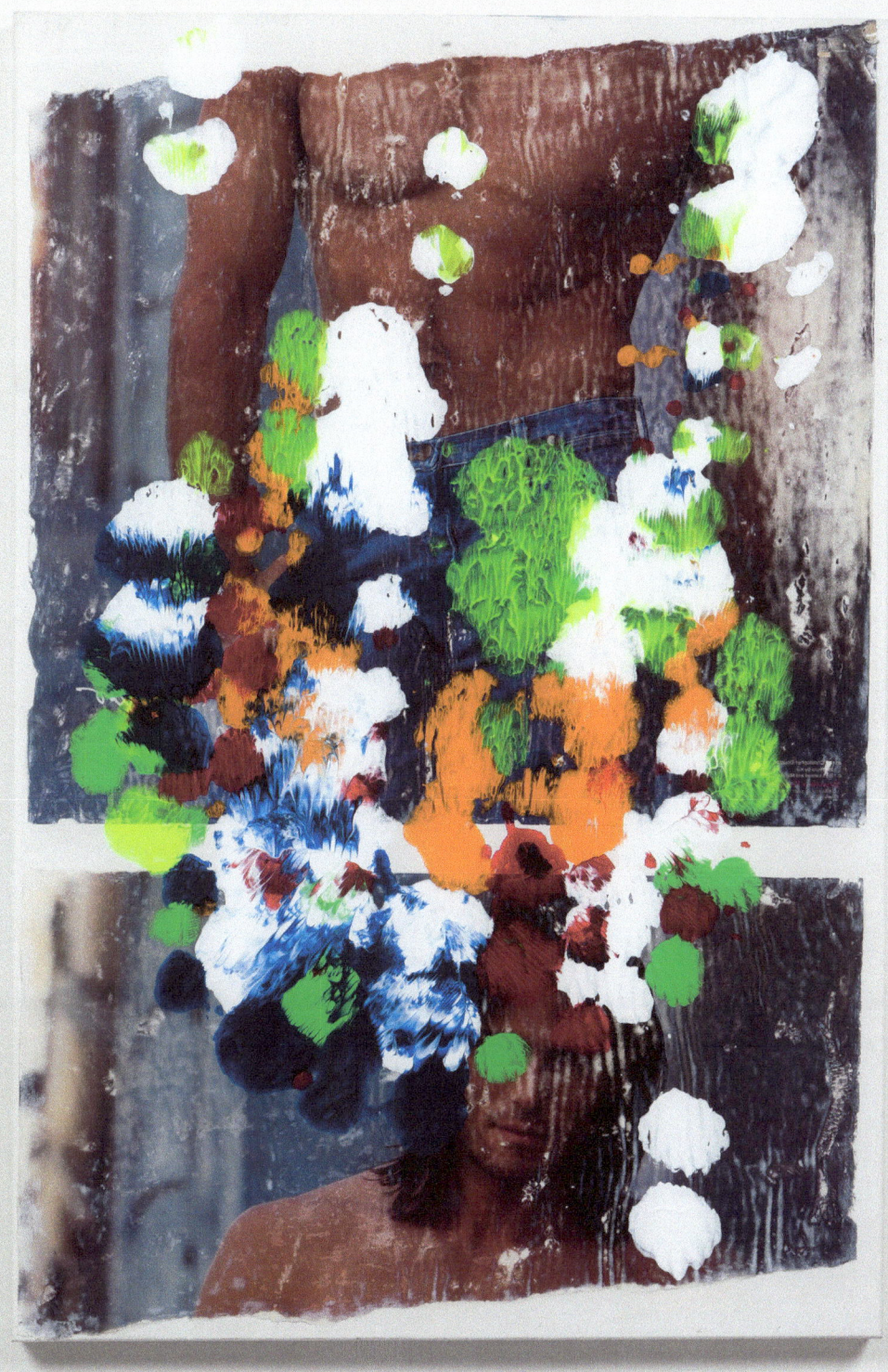

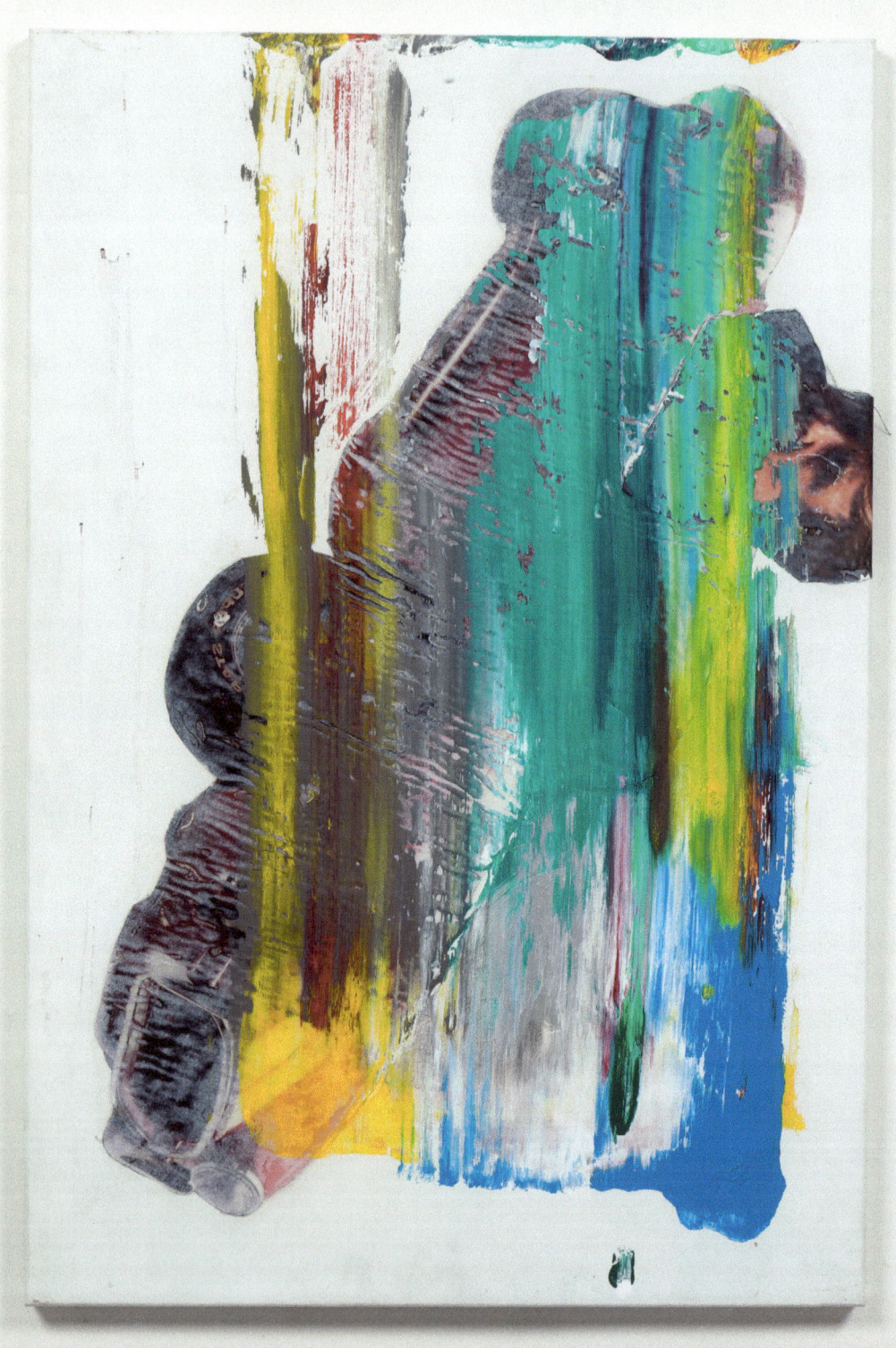

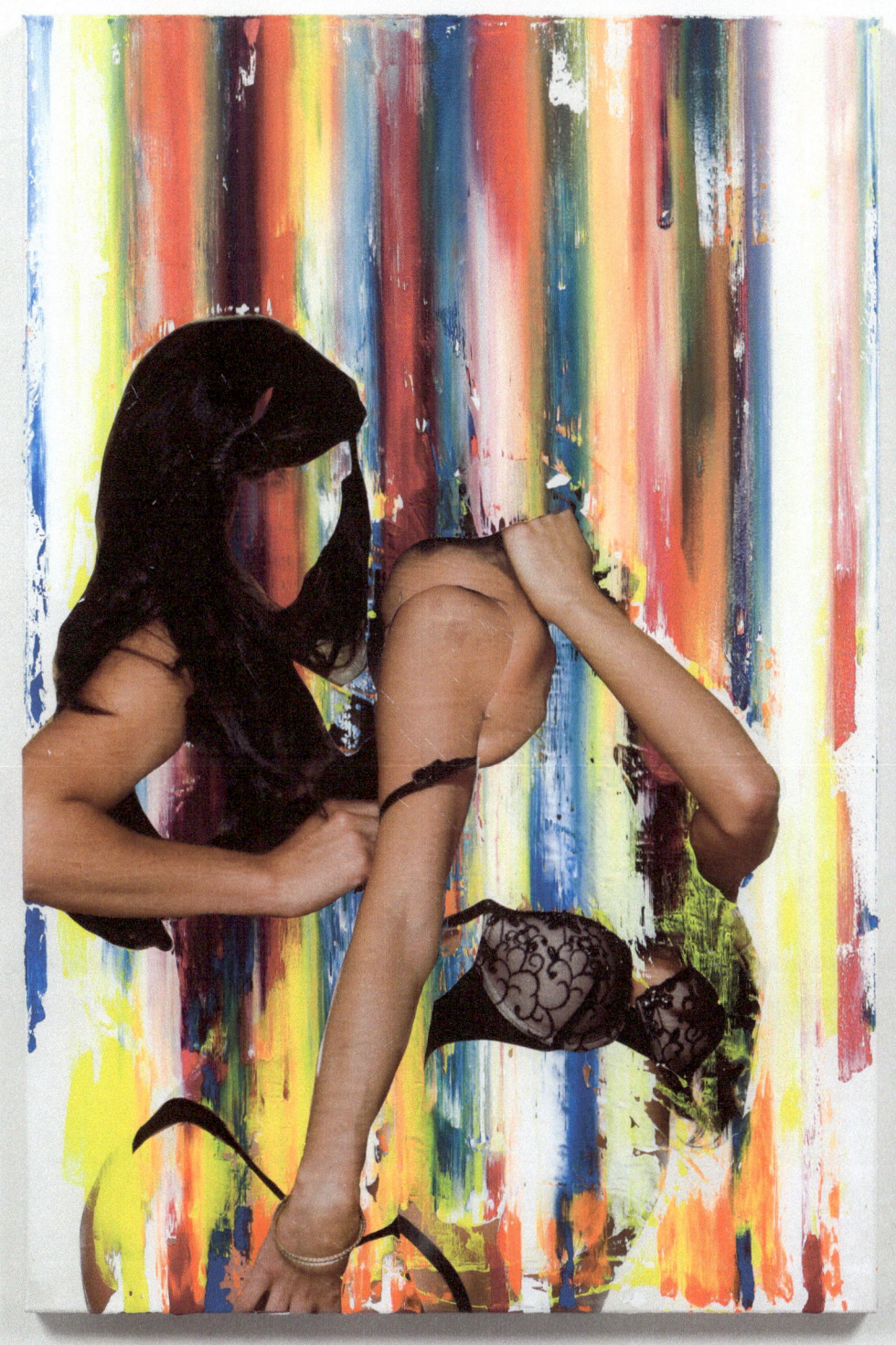

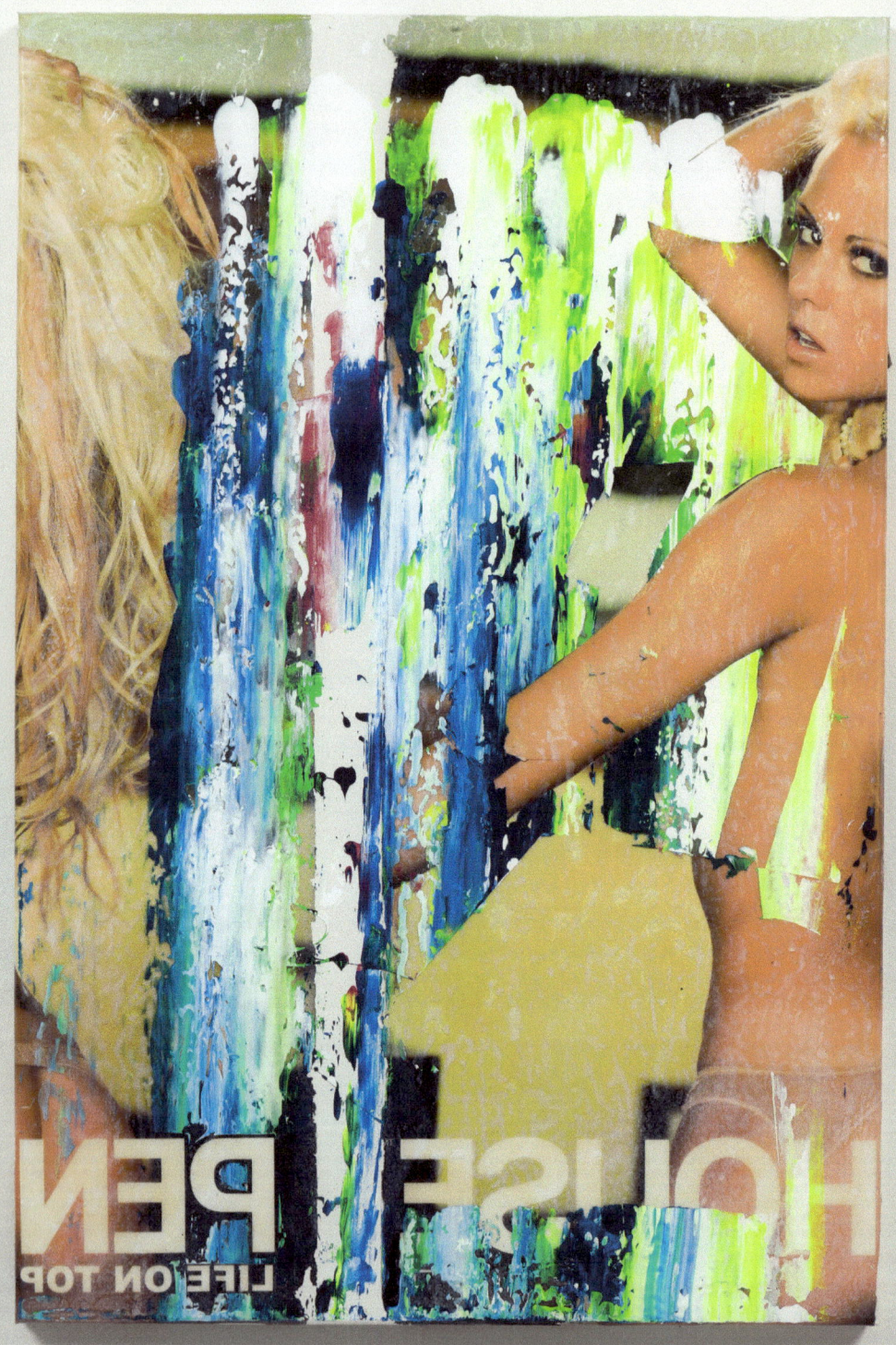

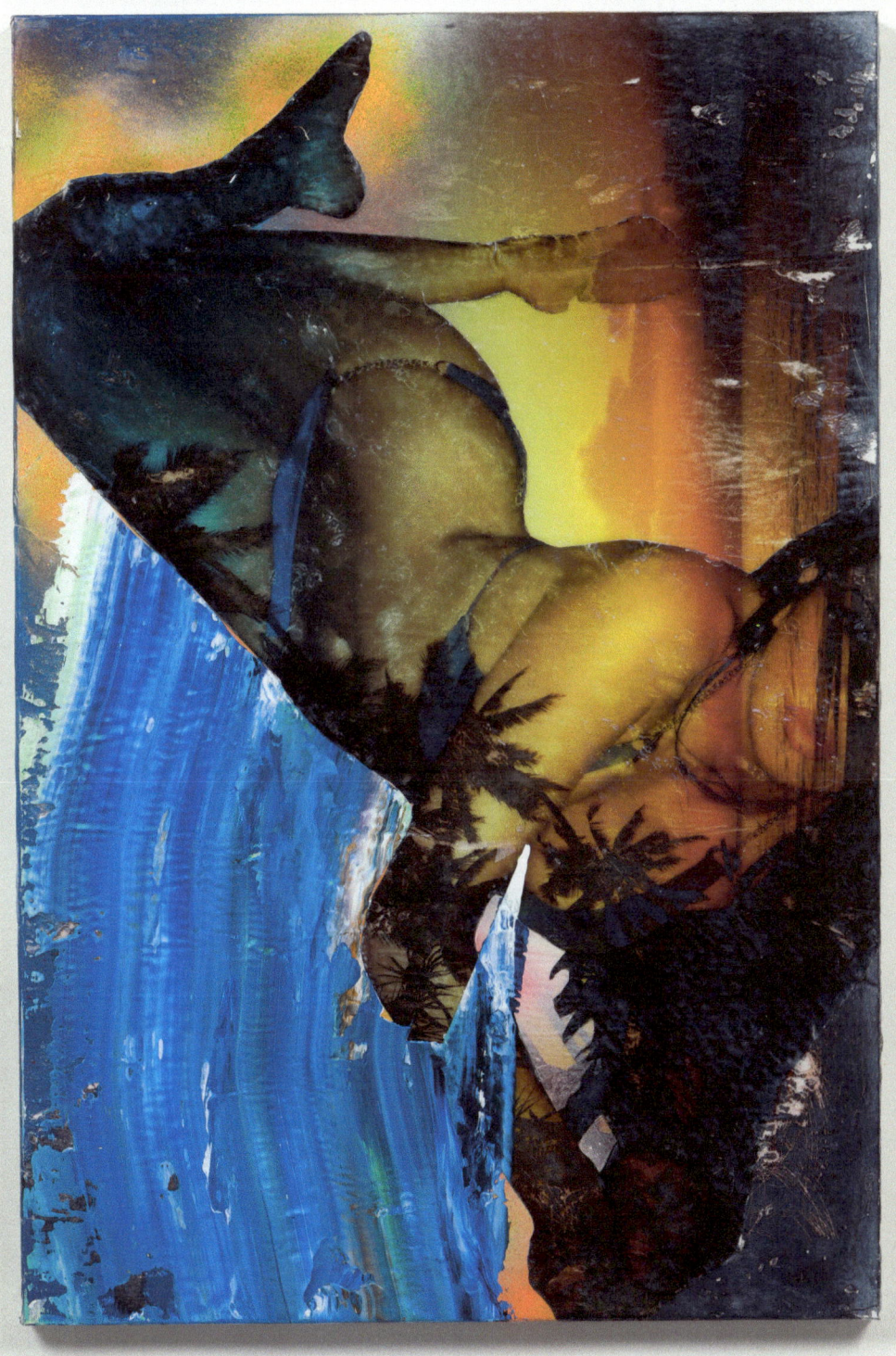

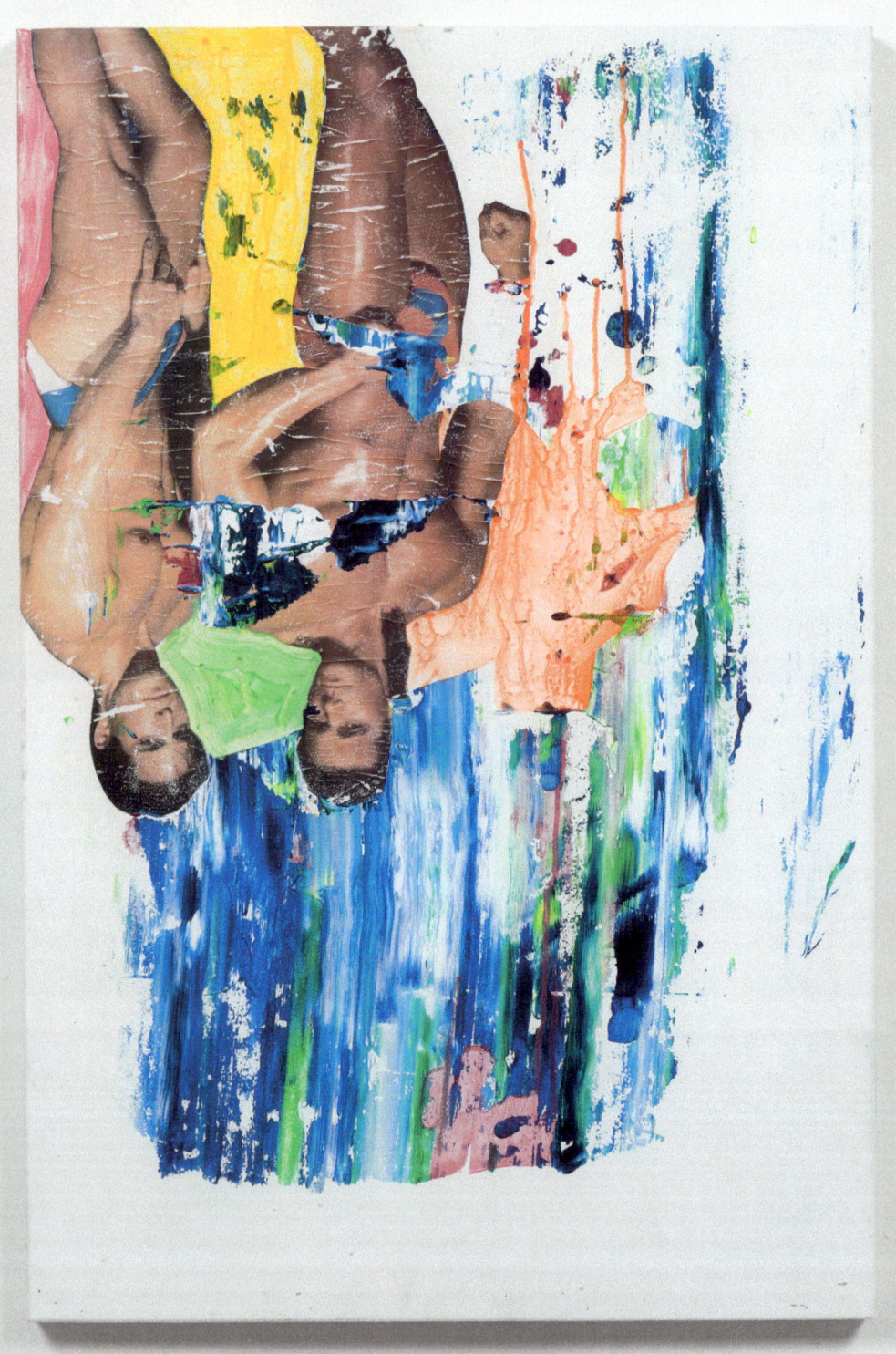

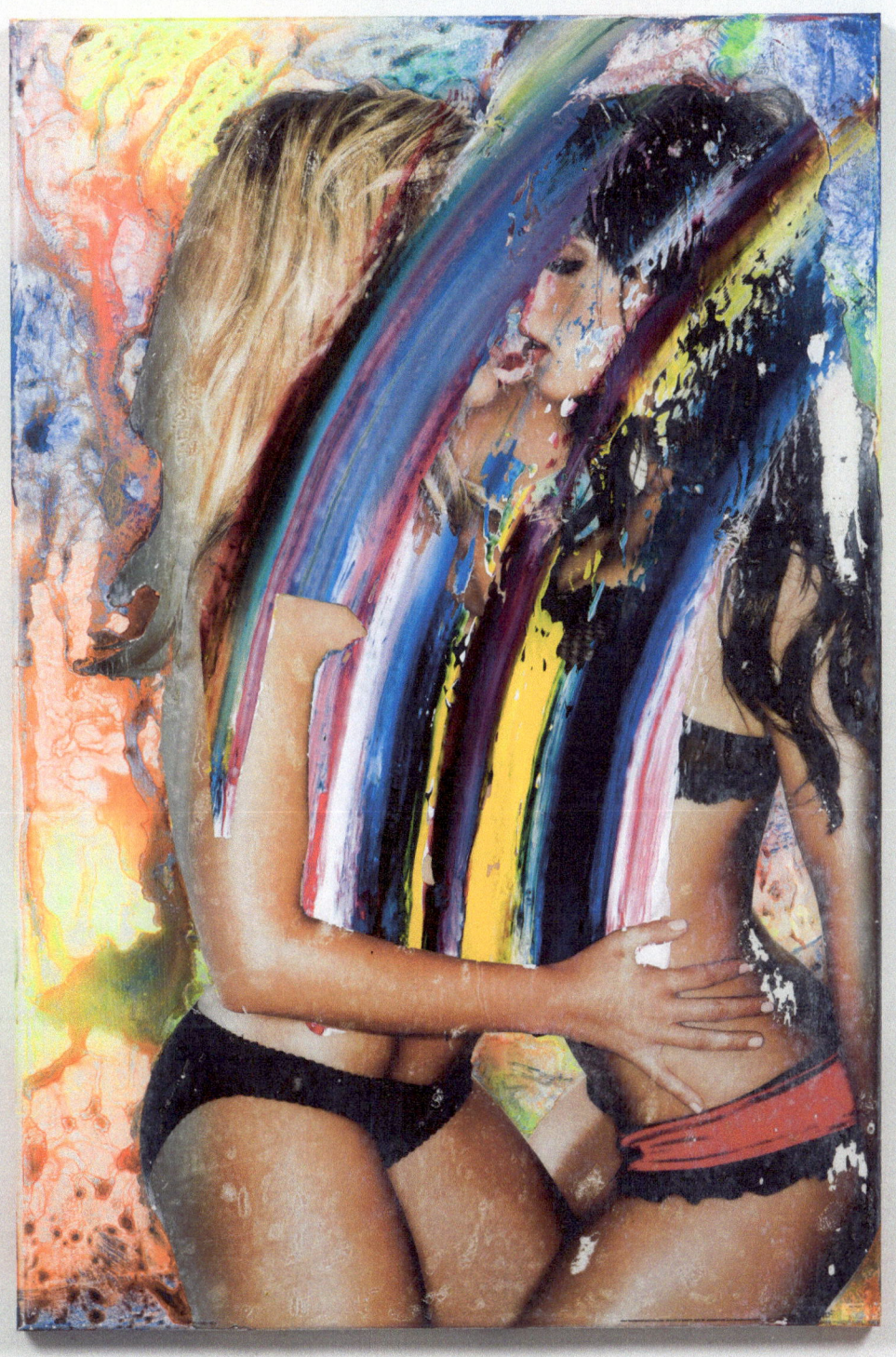

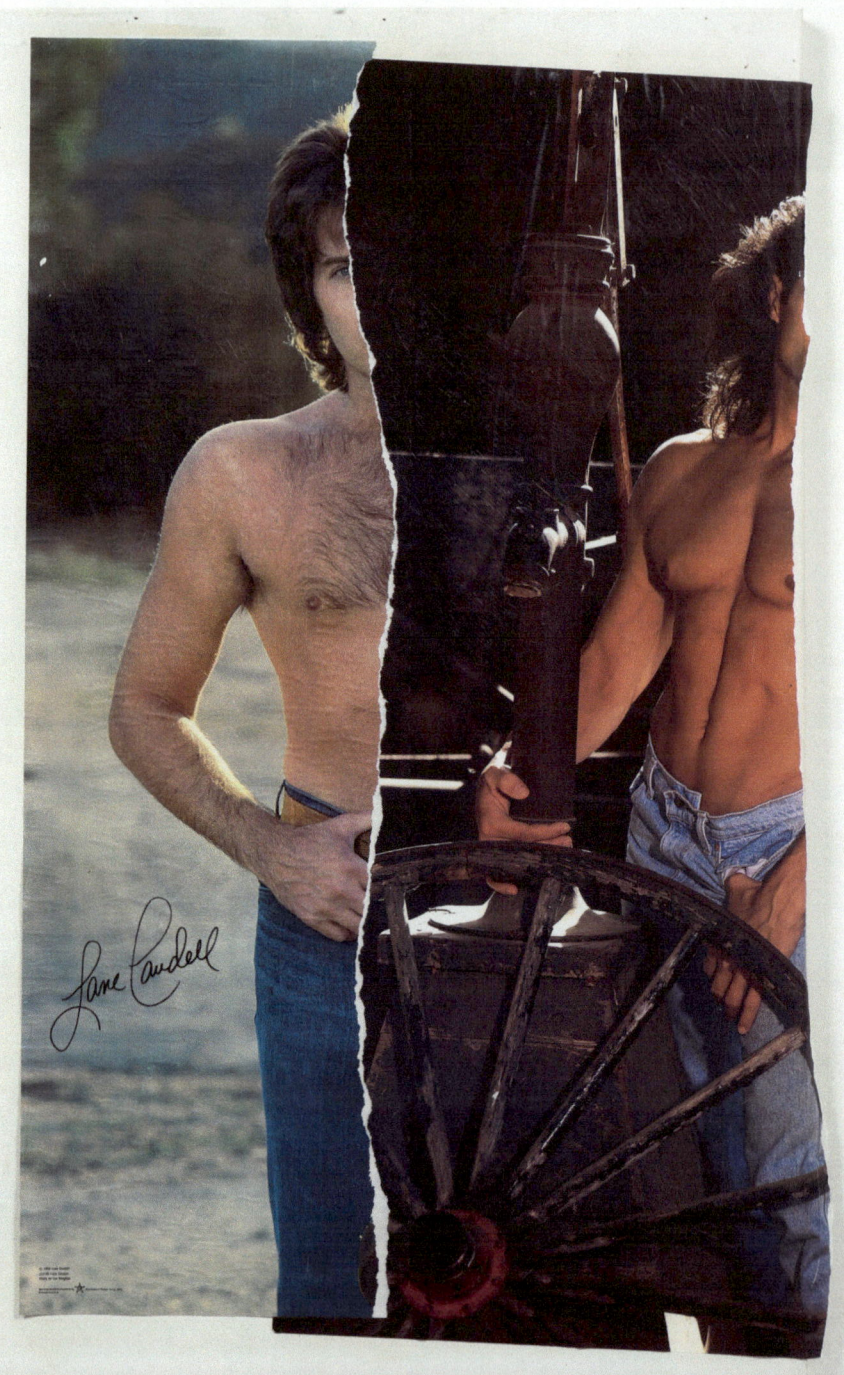

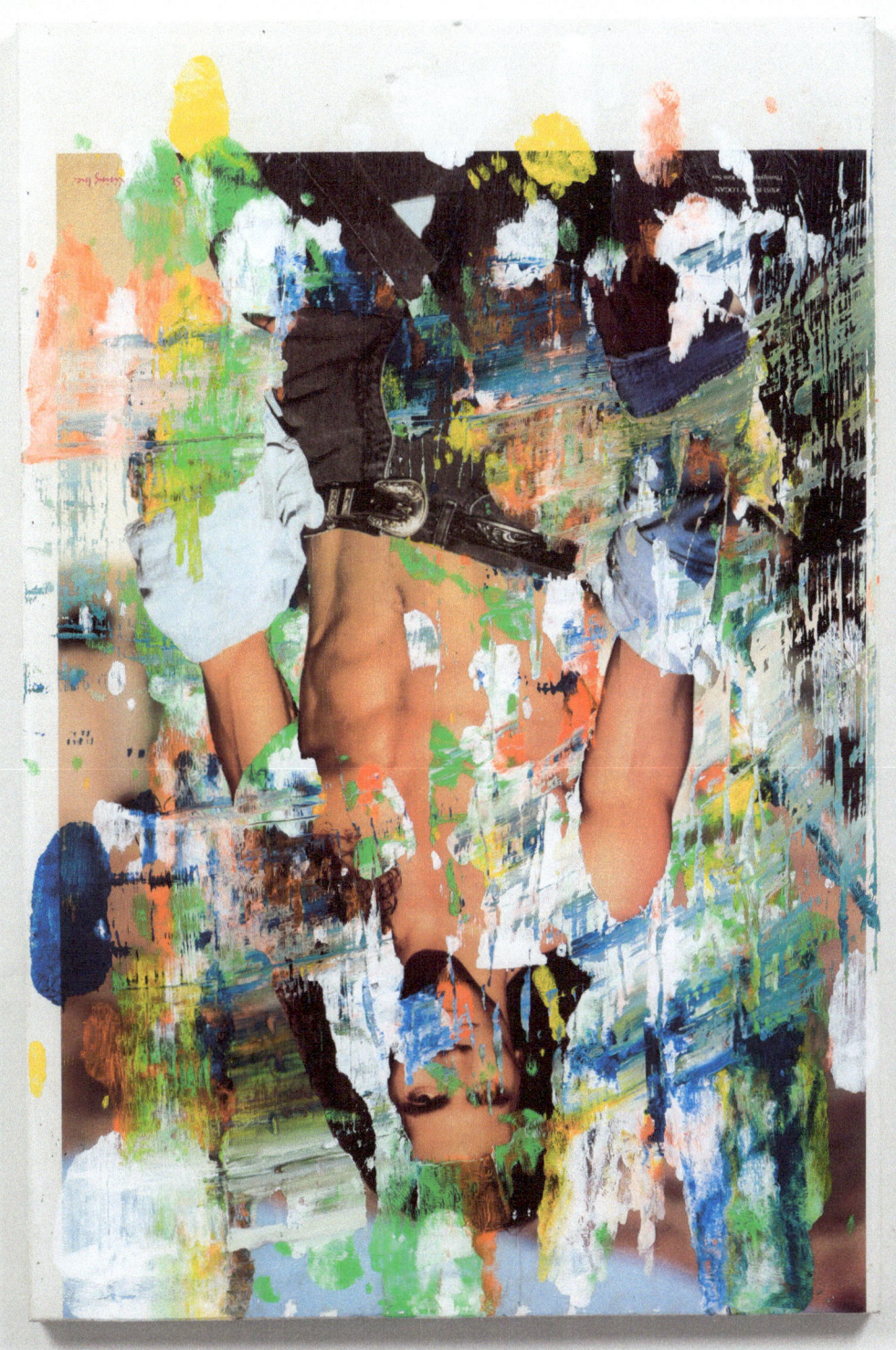

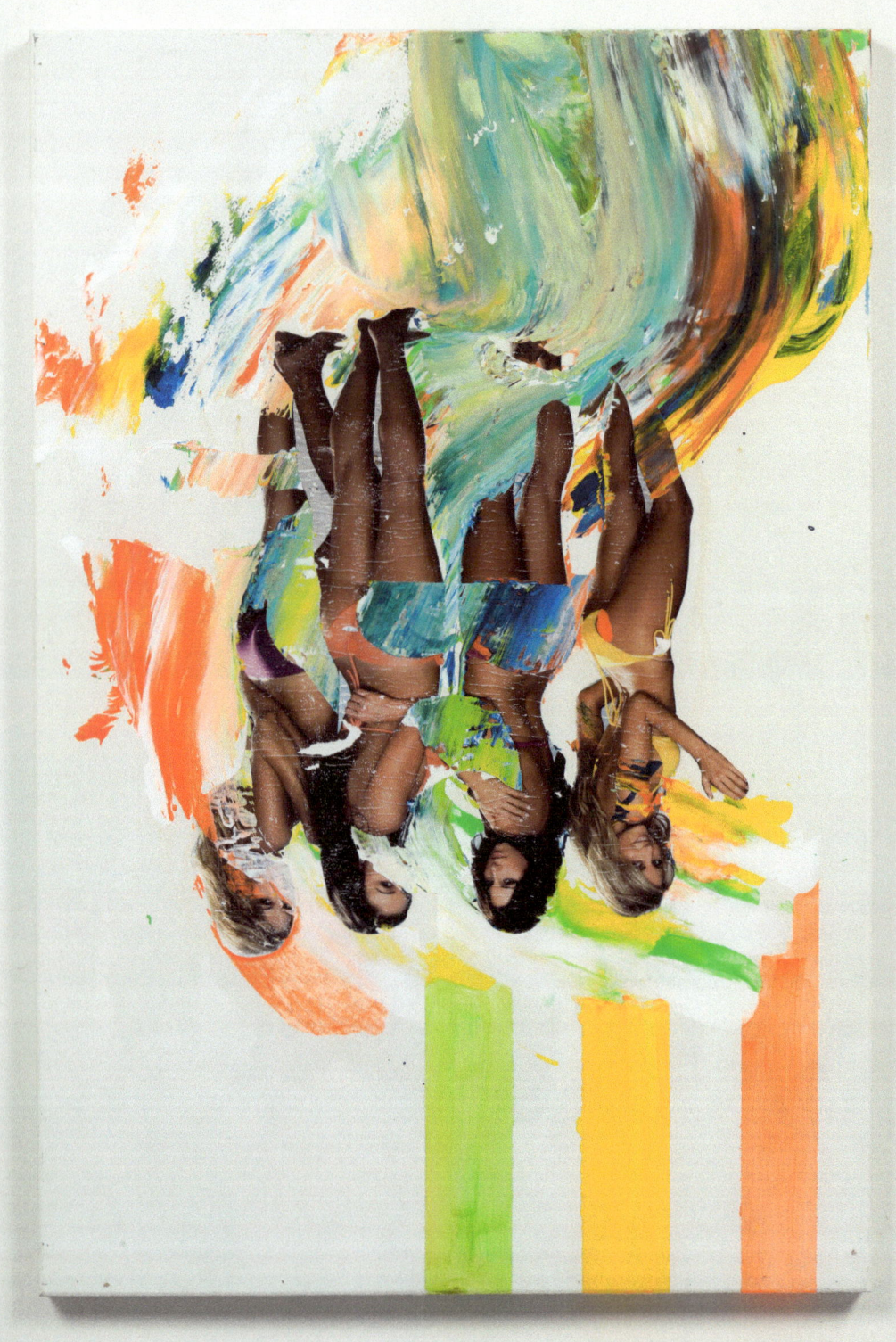

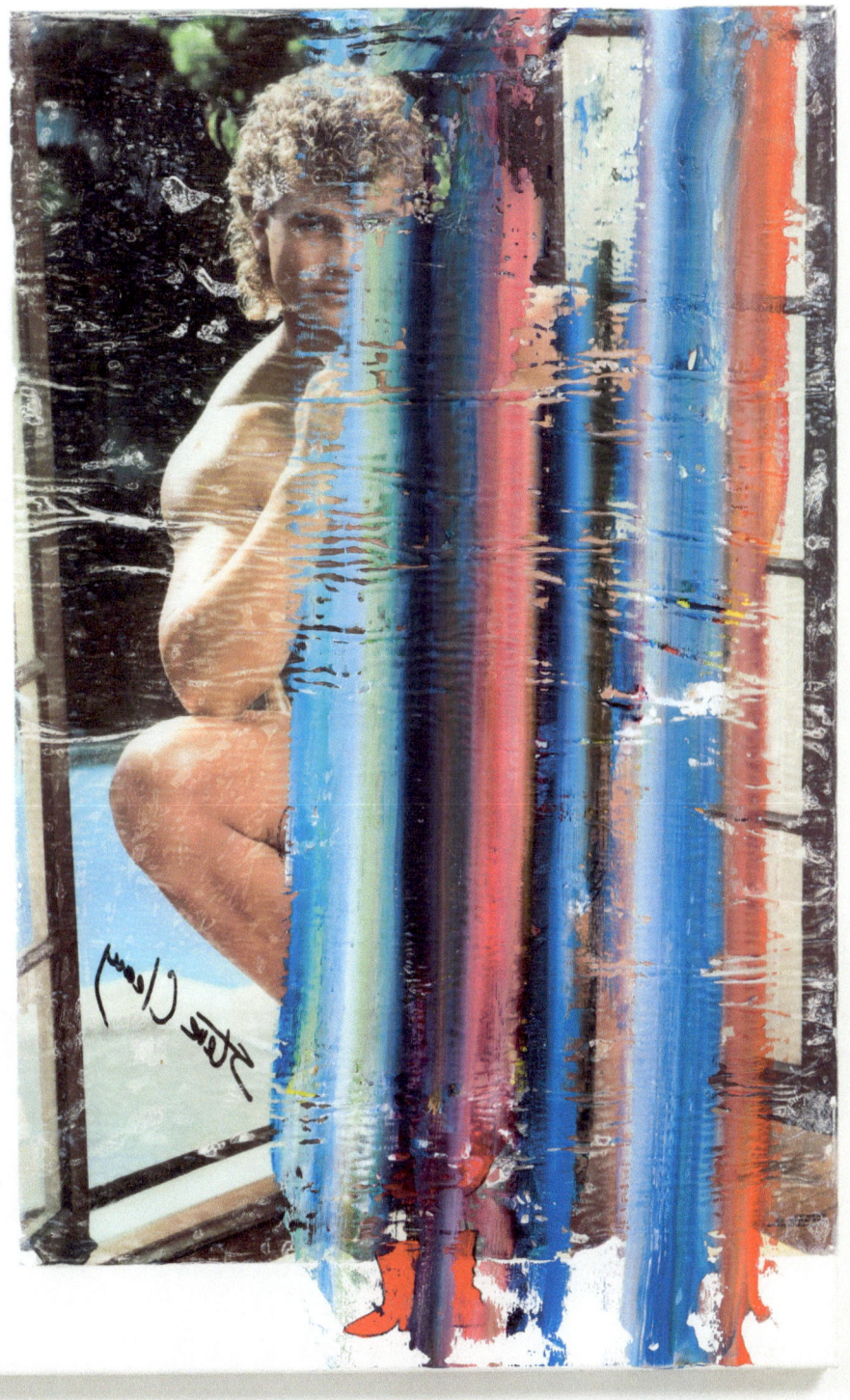

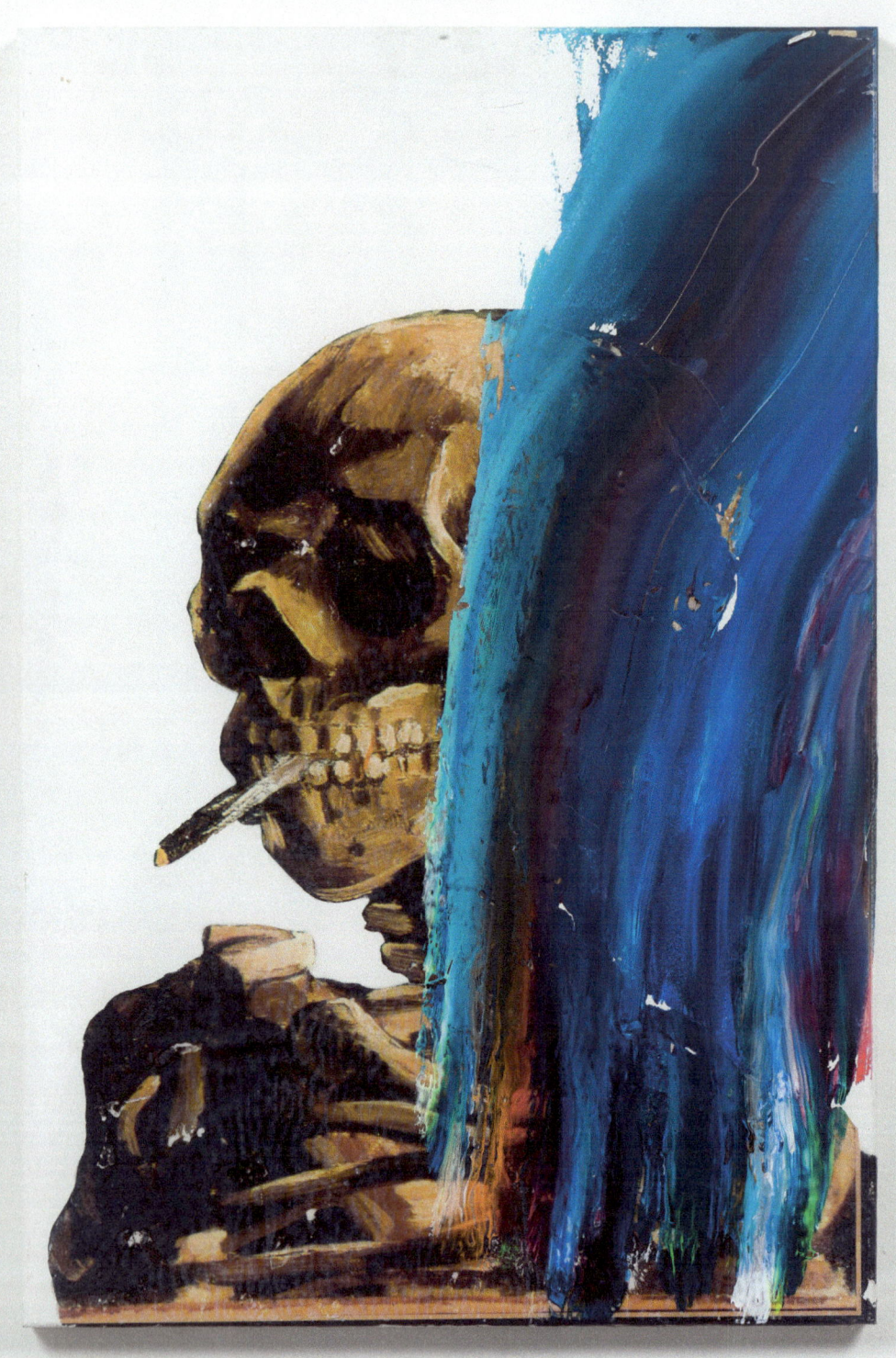

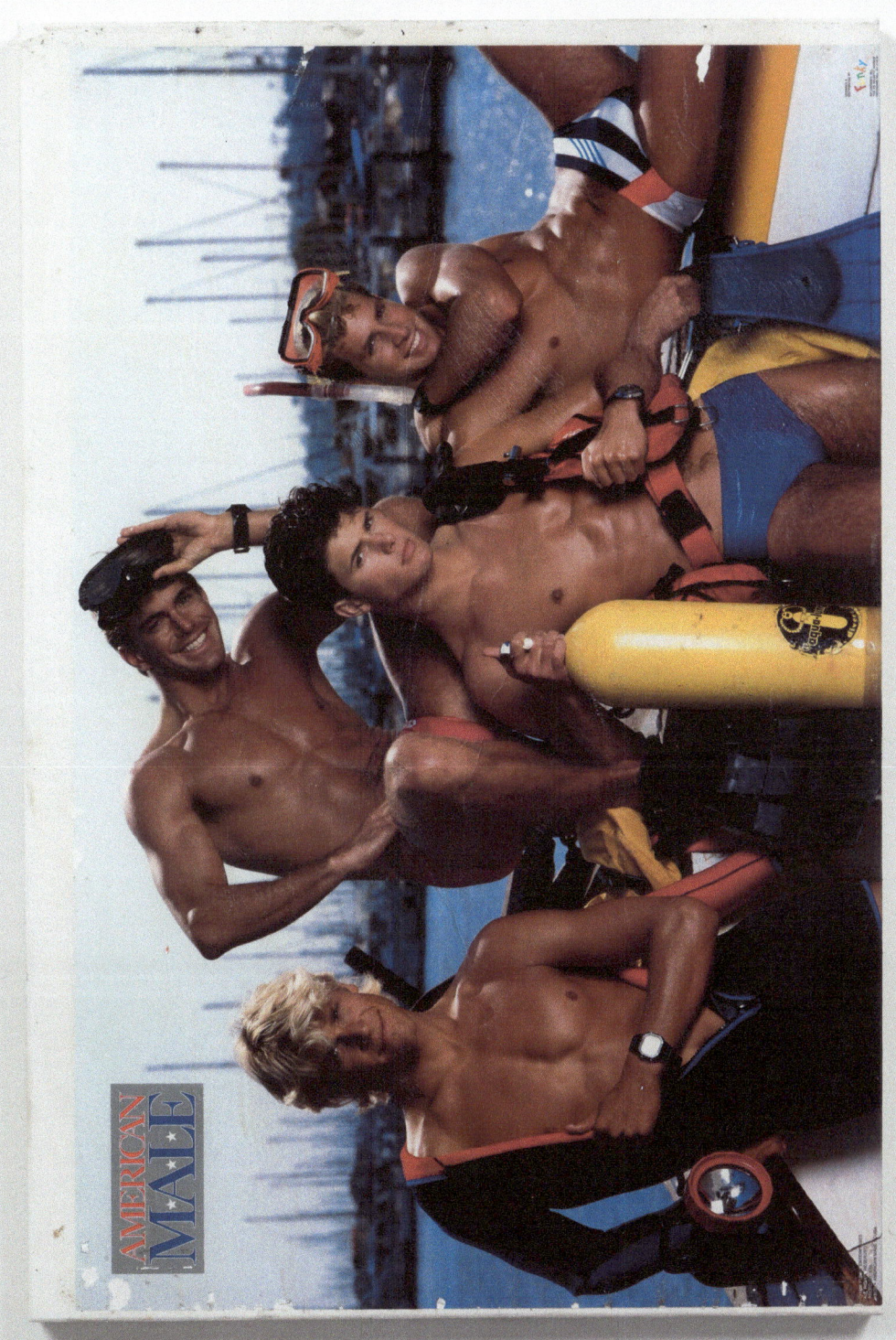

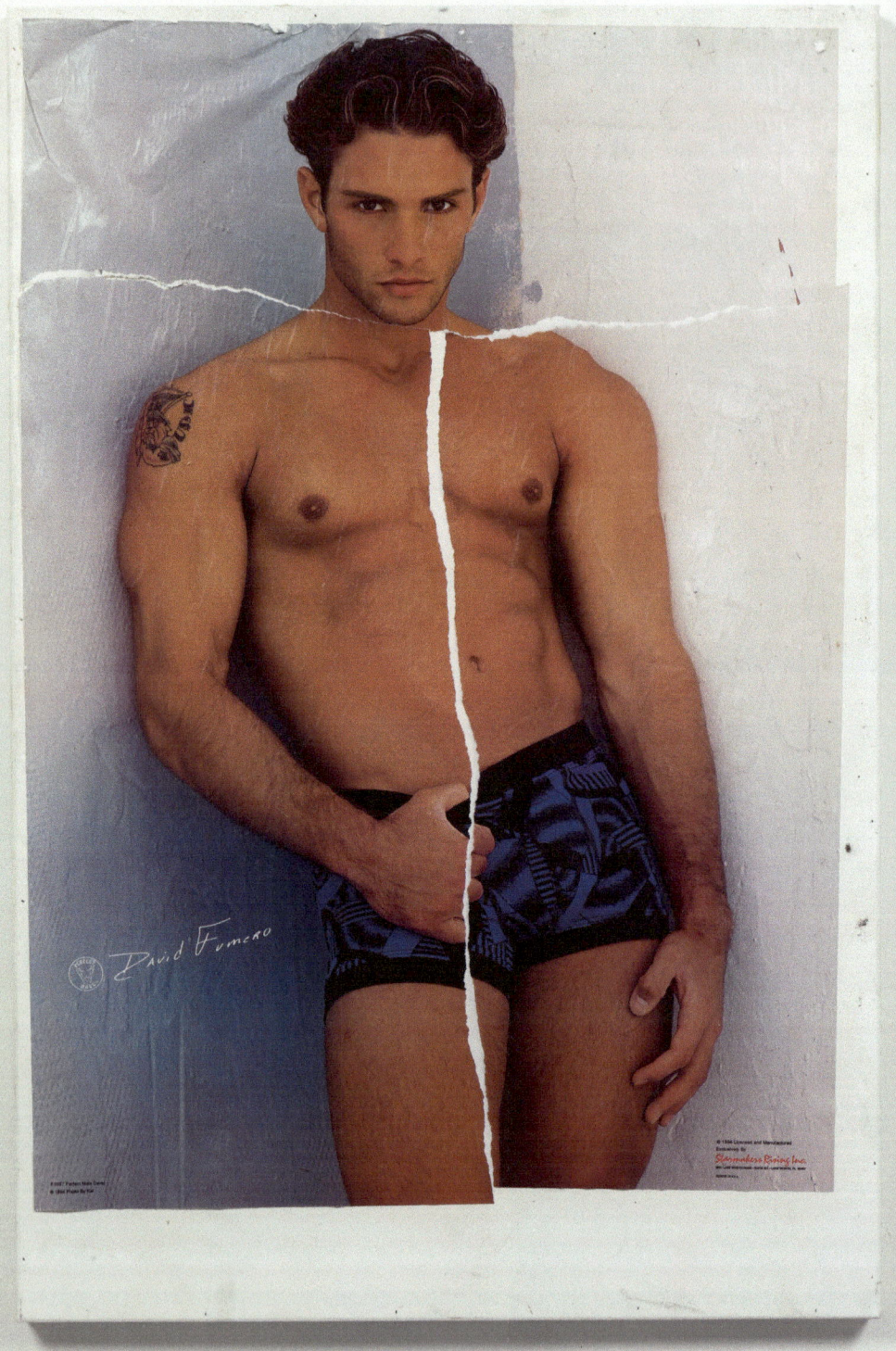

David Fumero

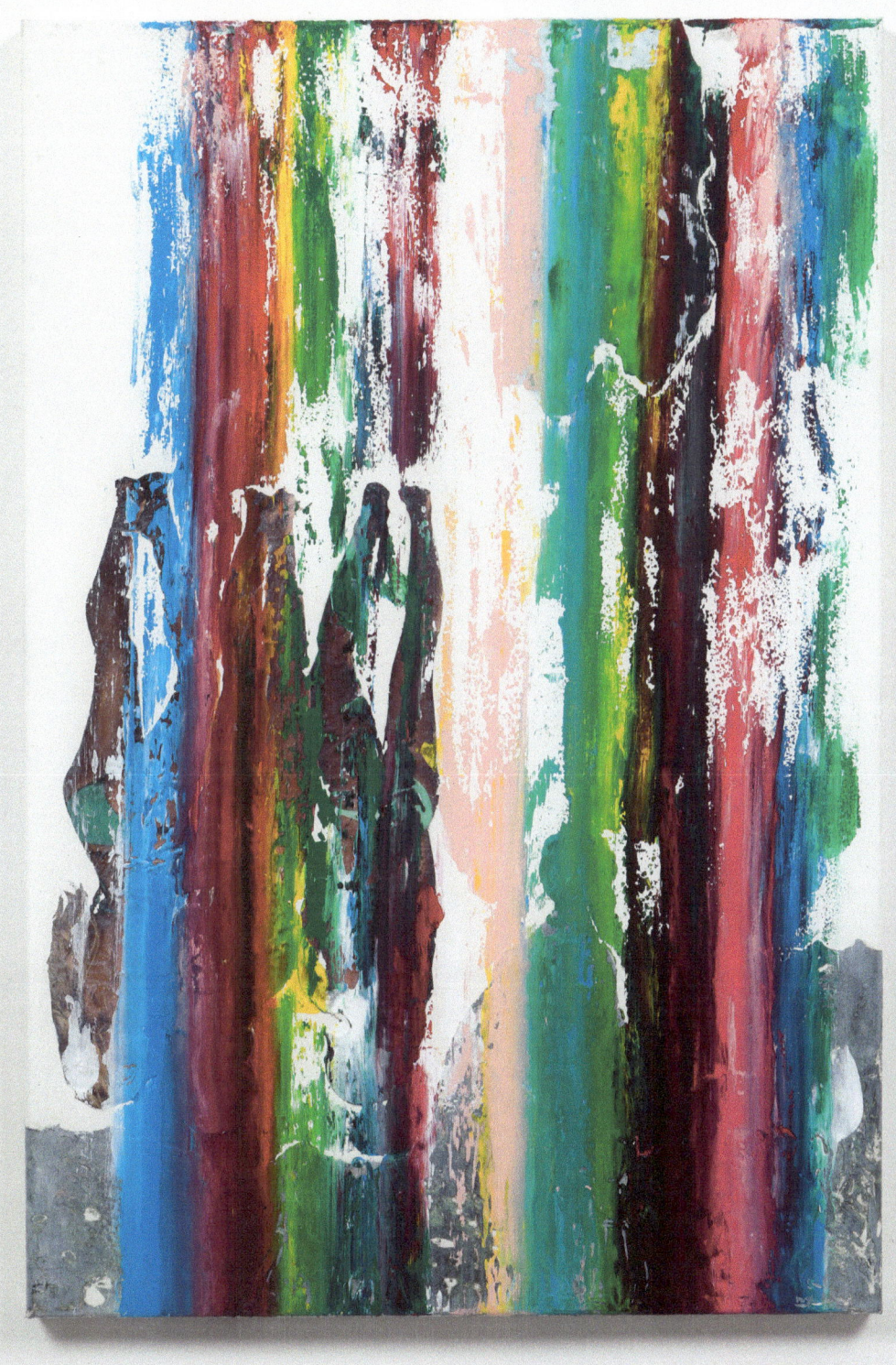

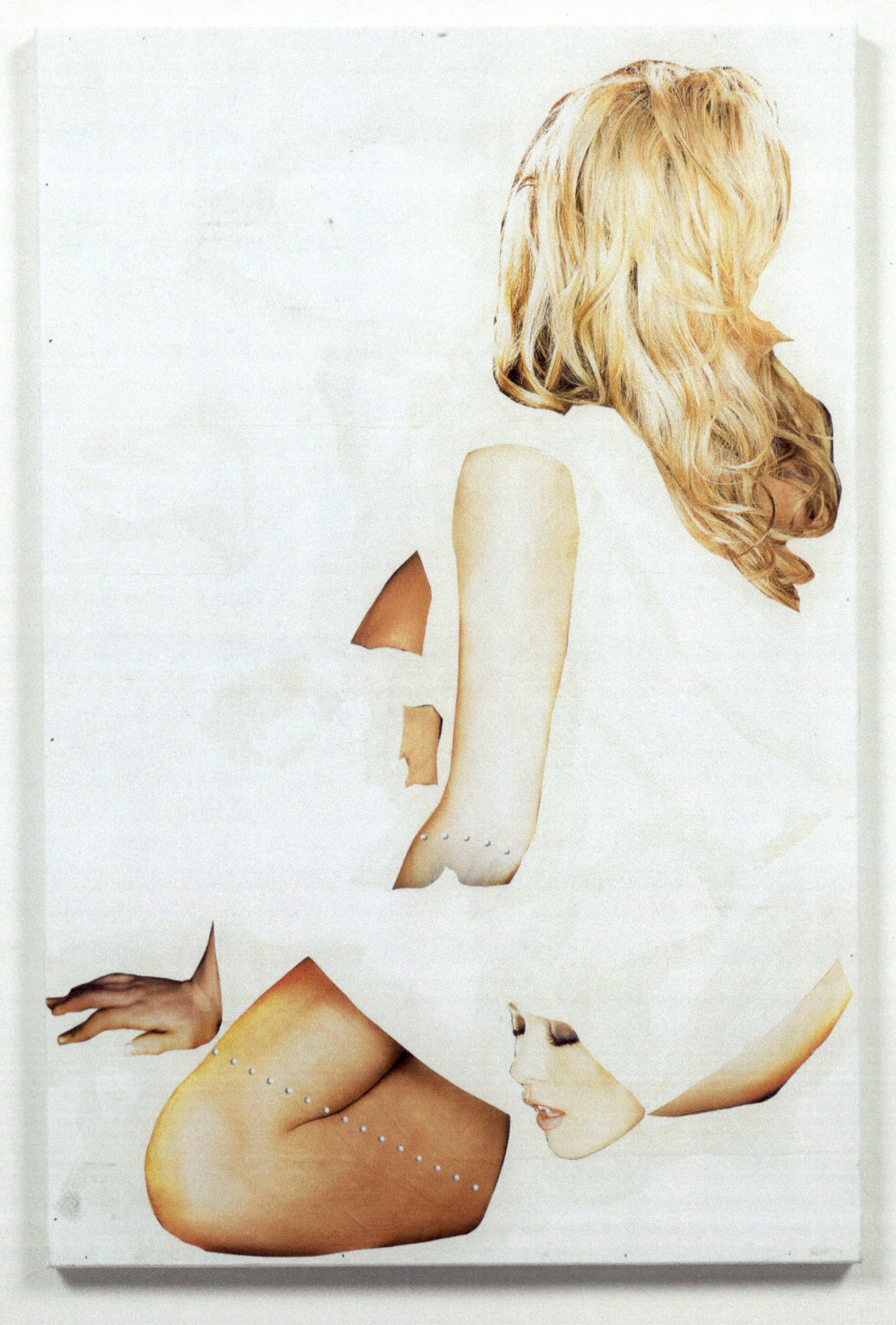

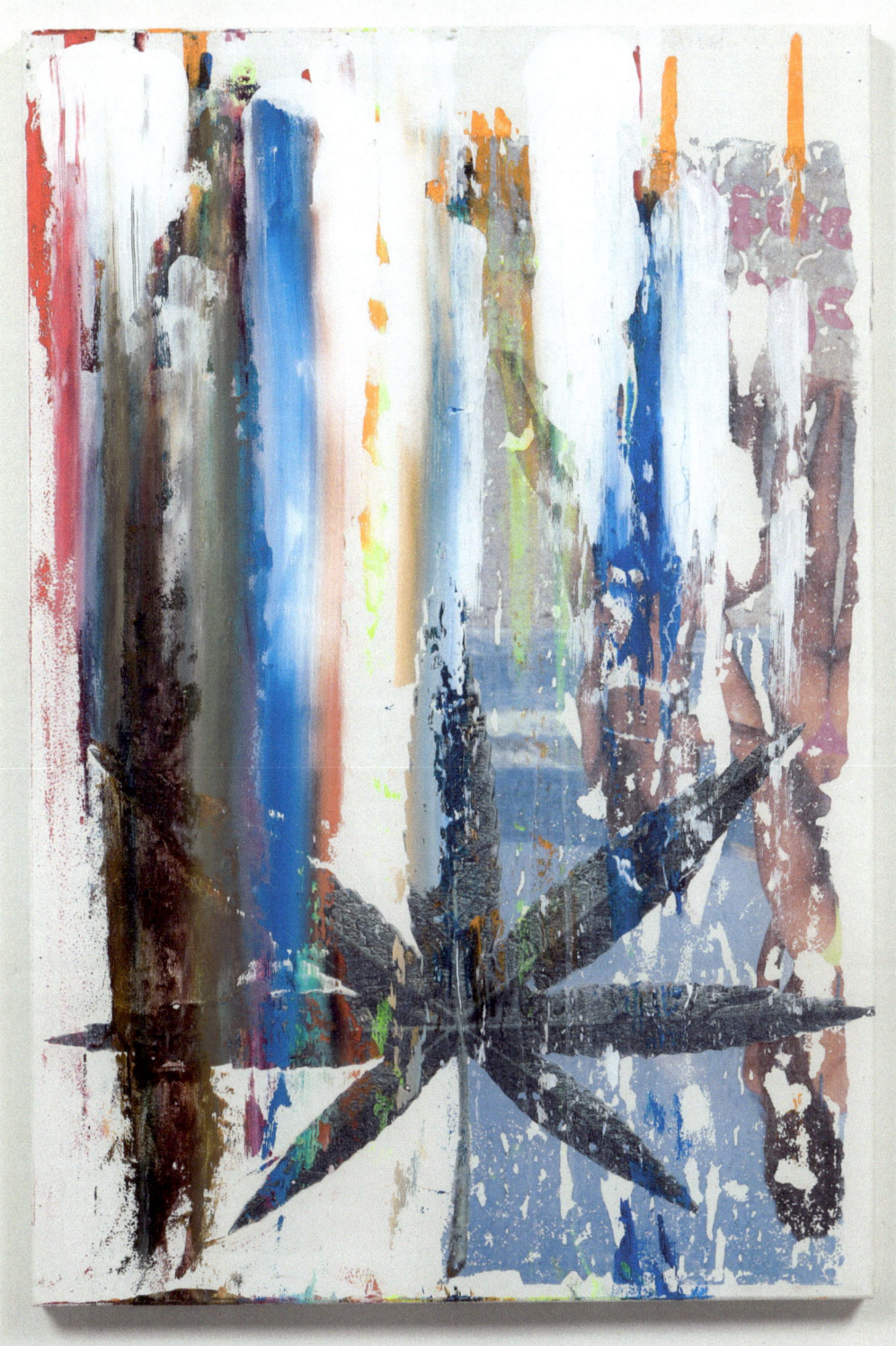

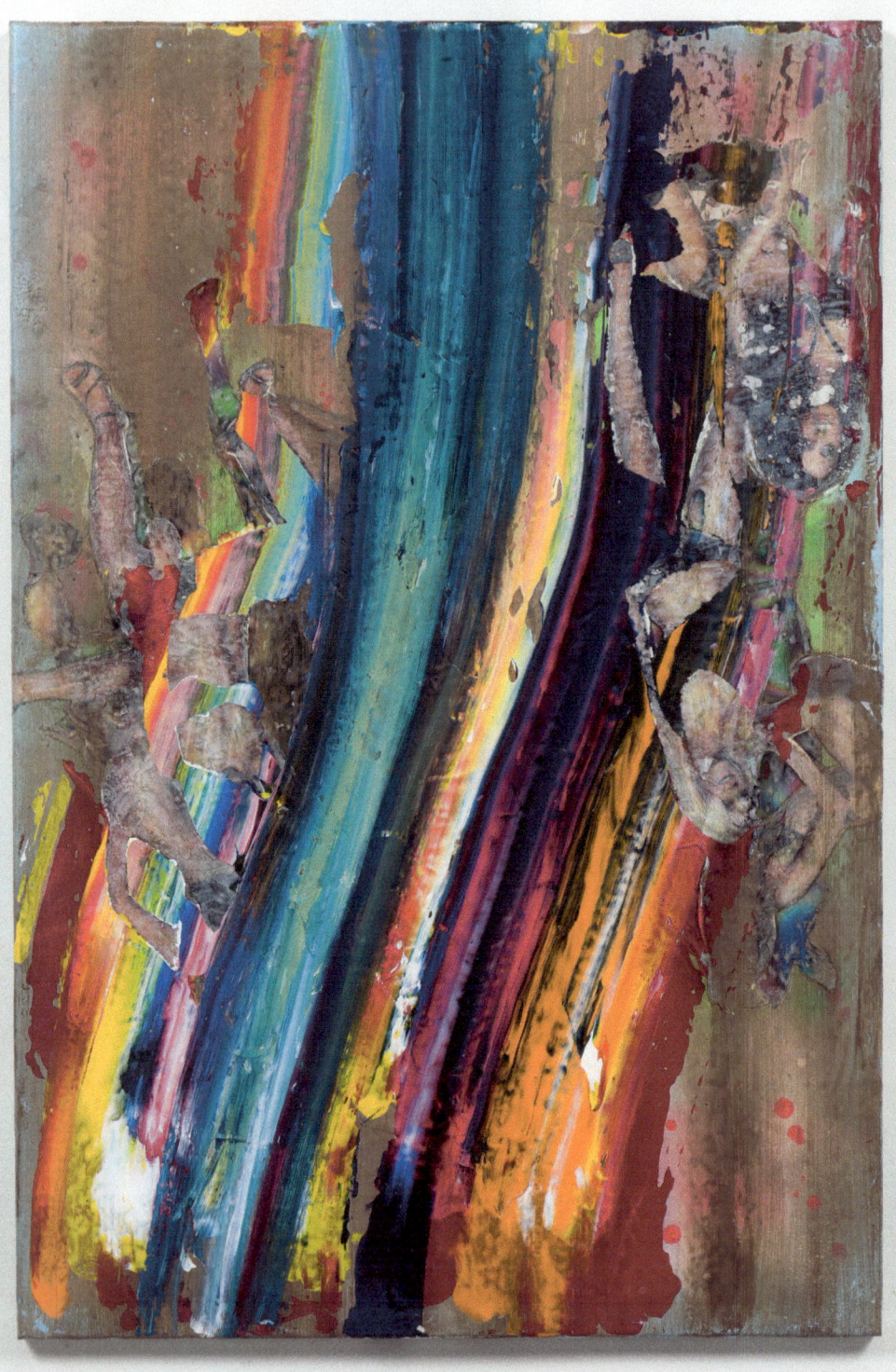

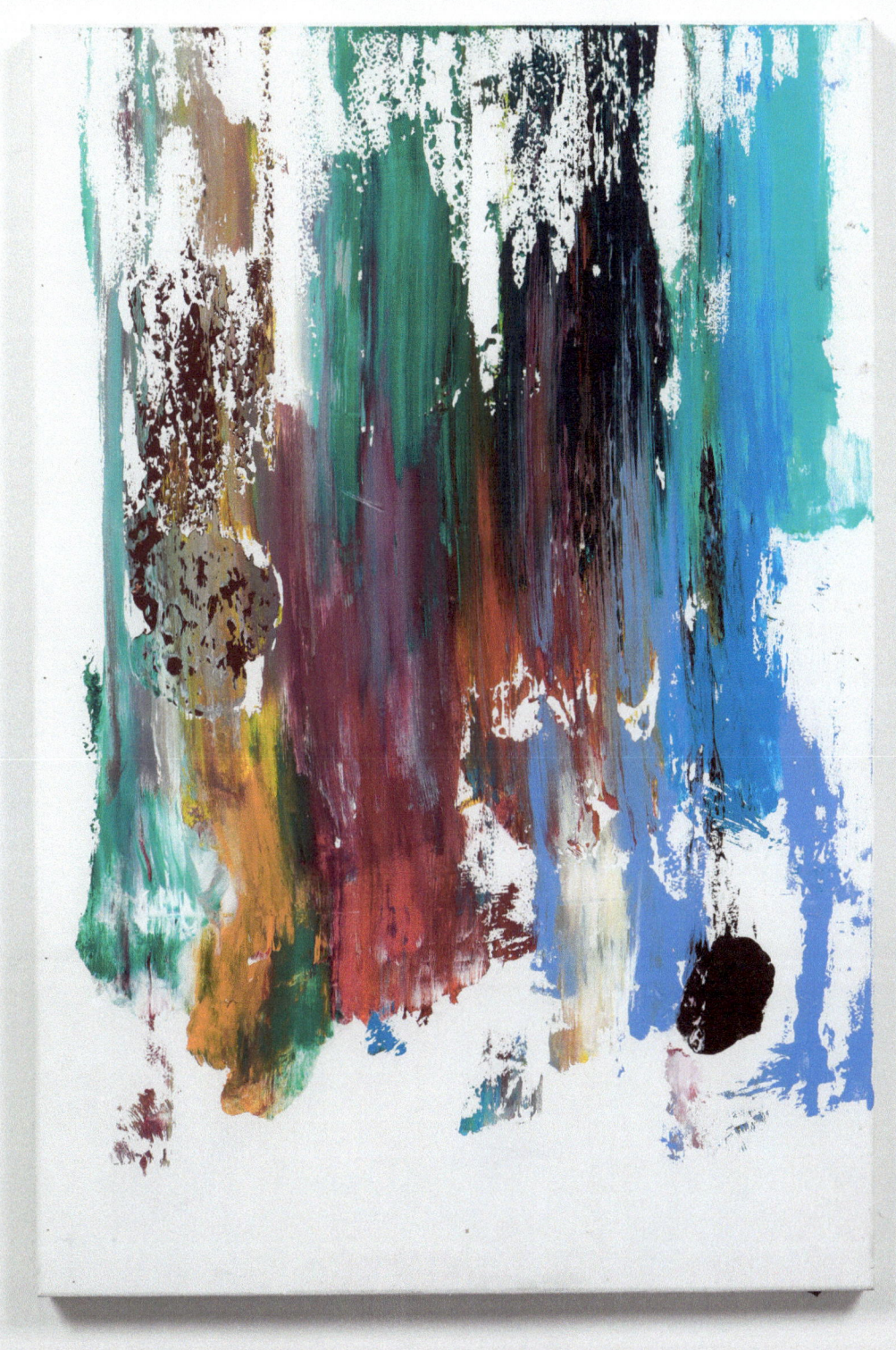

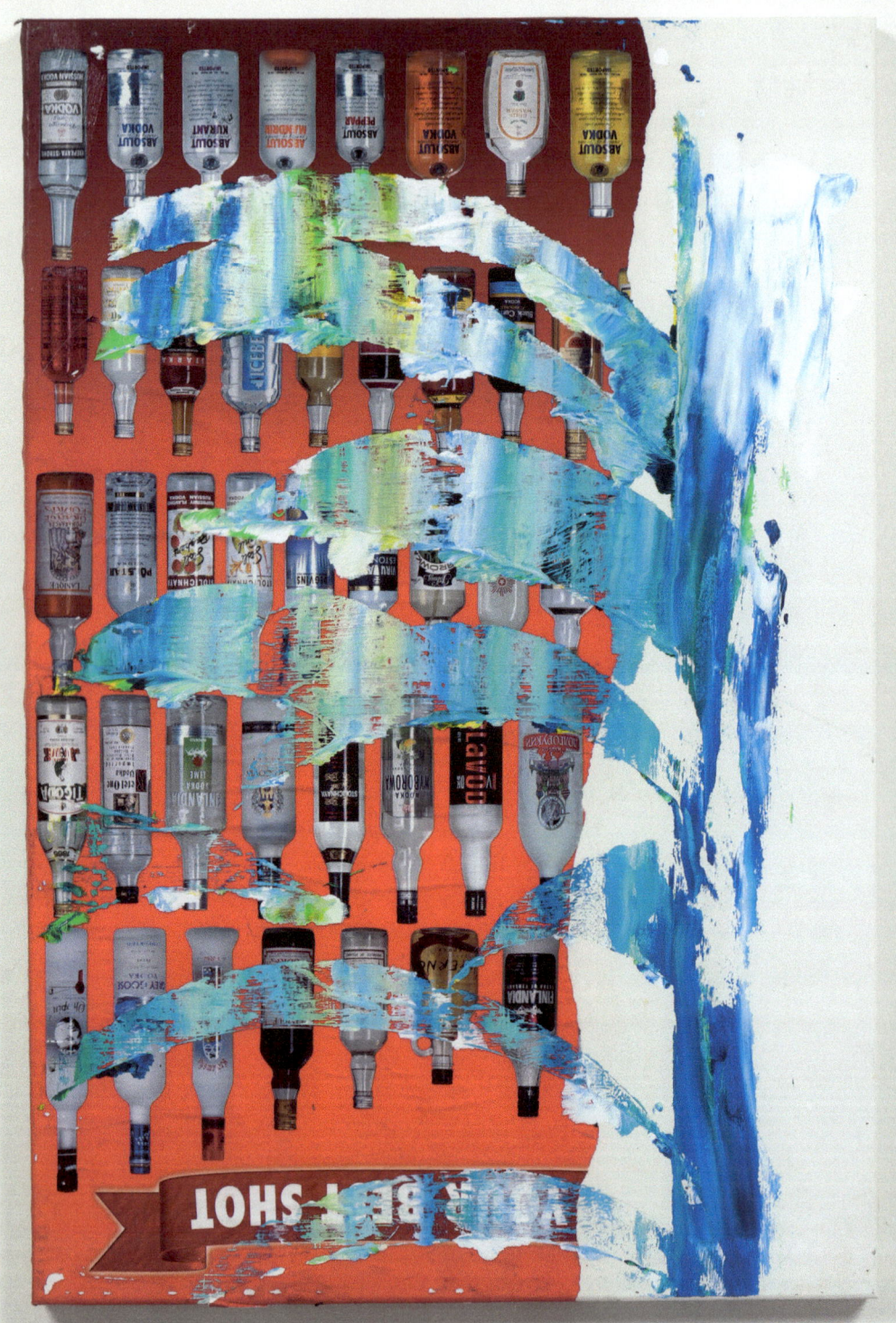

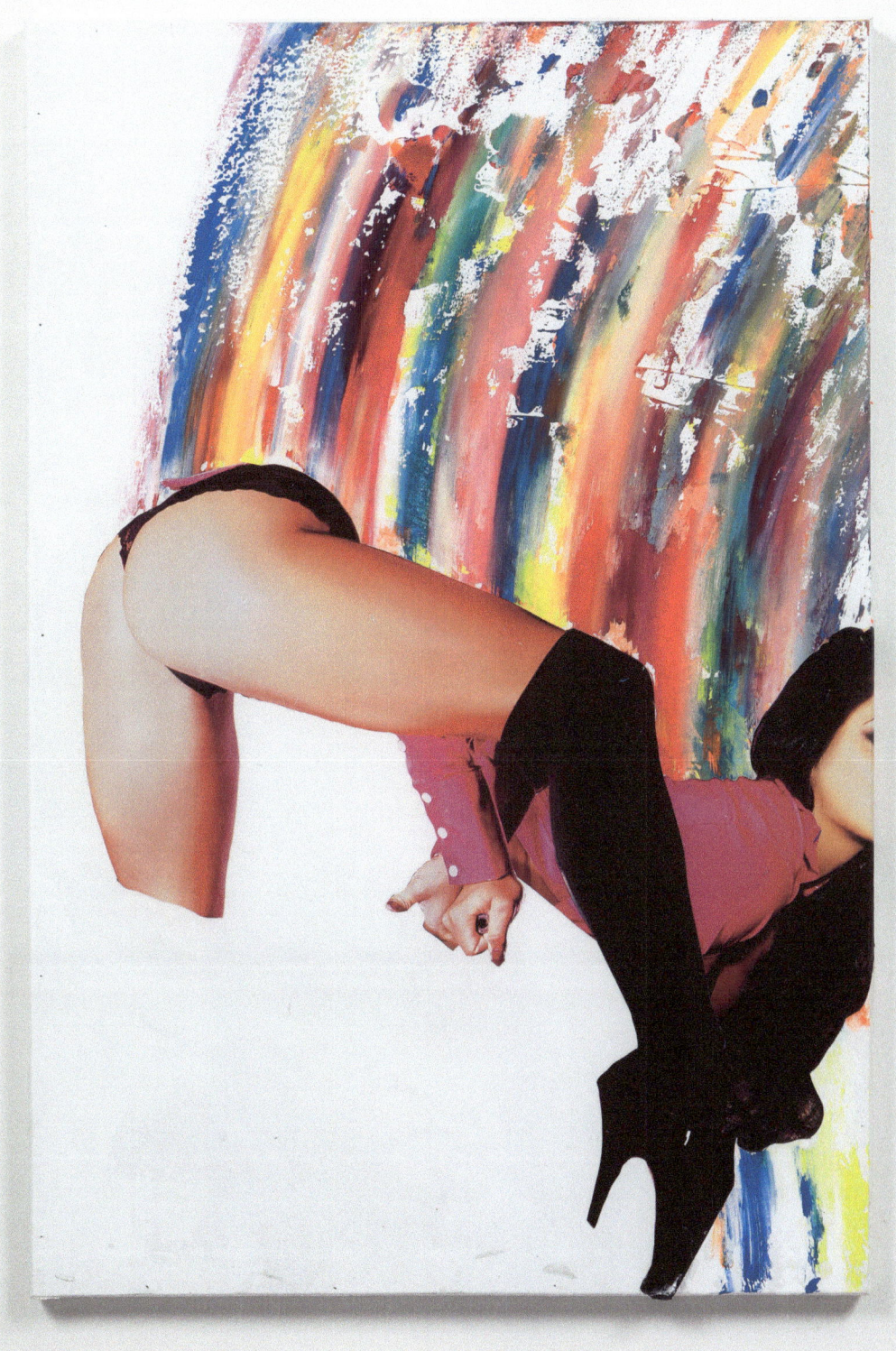

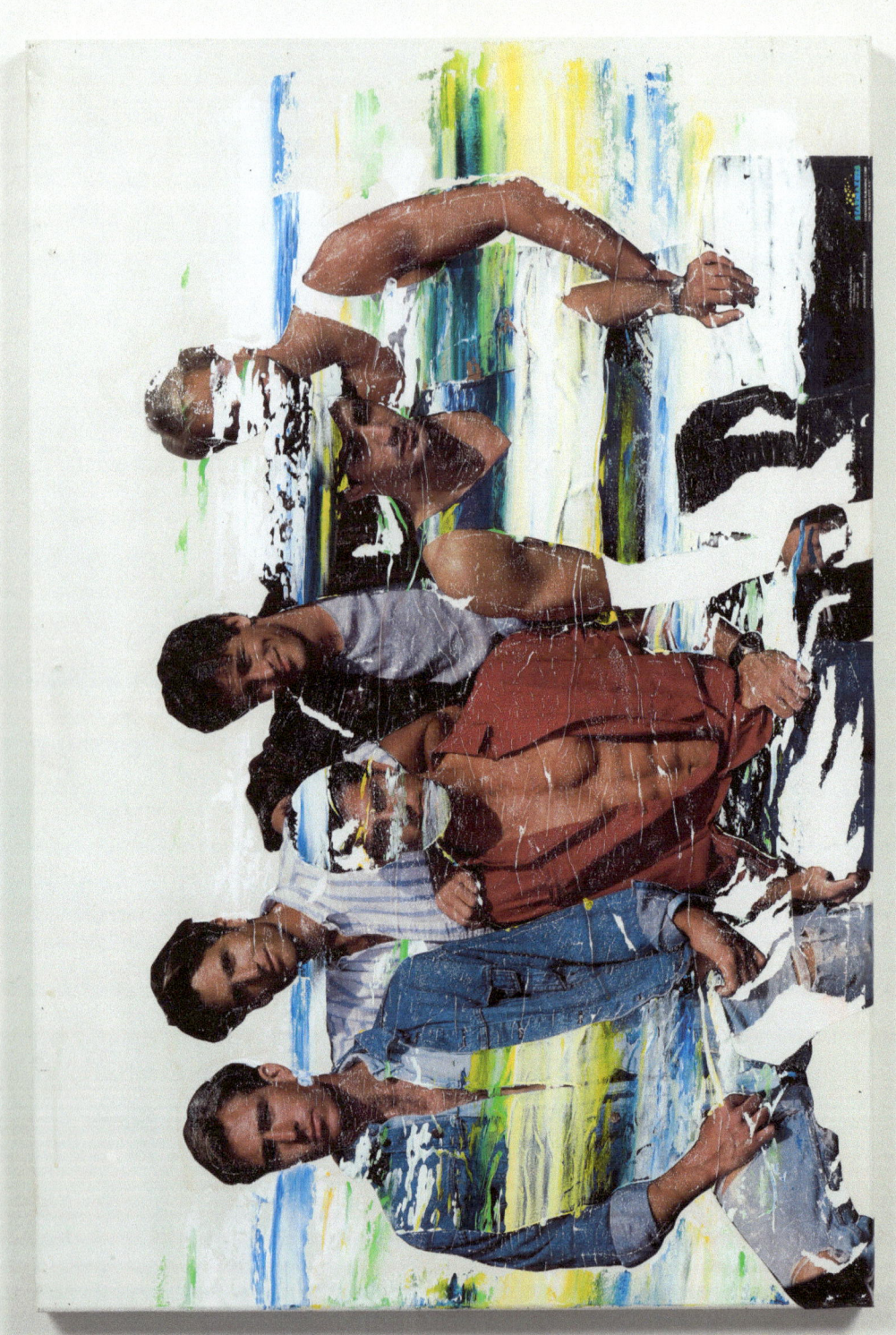

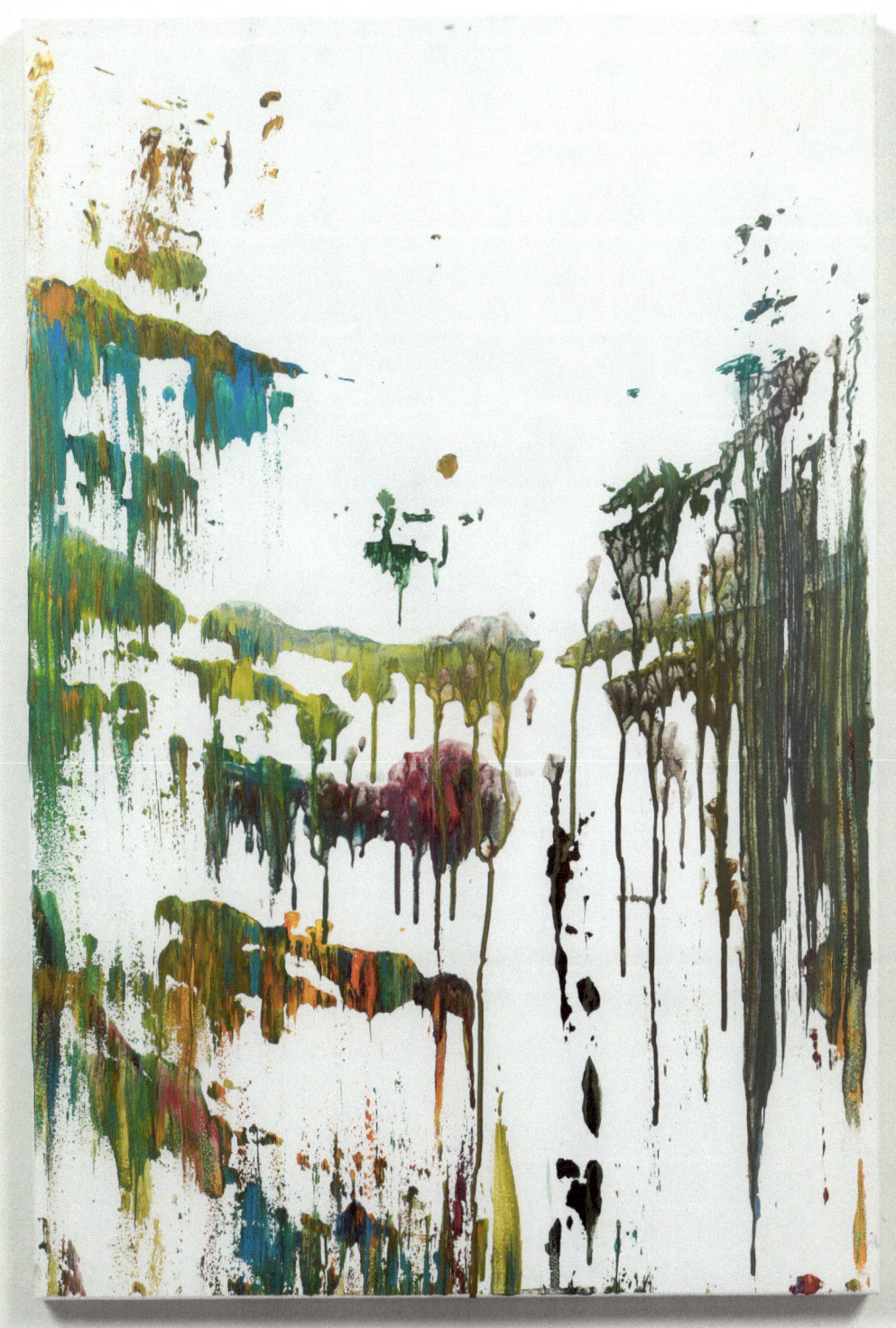

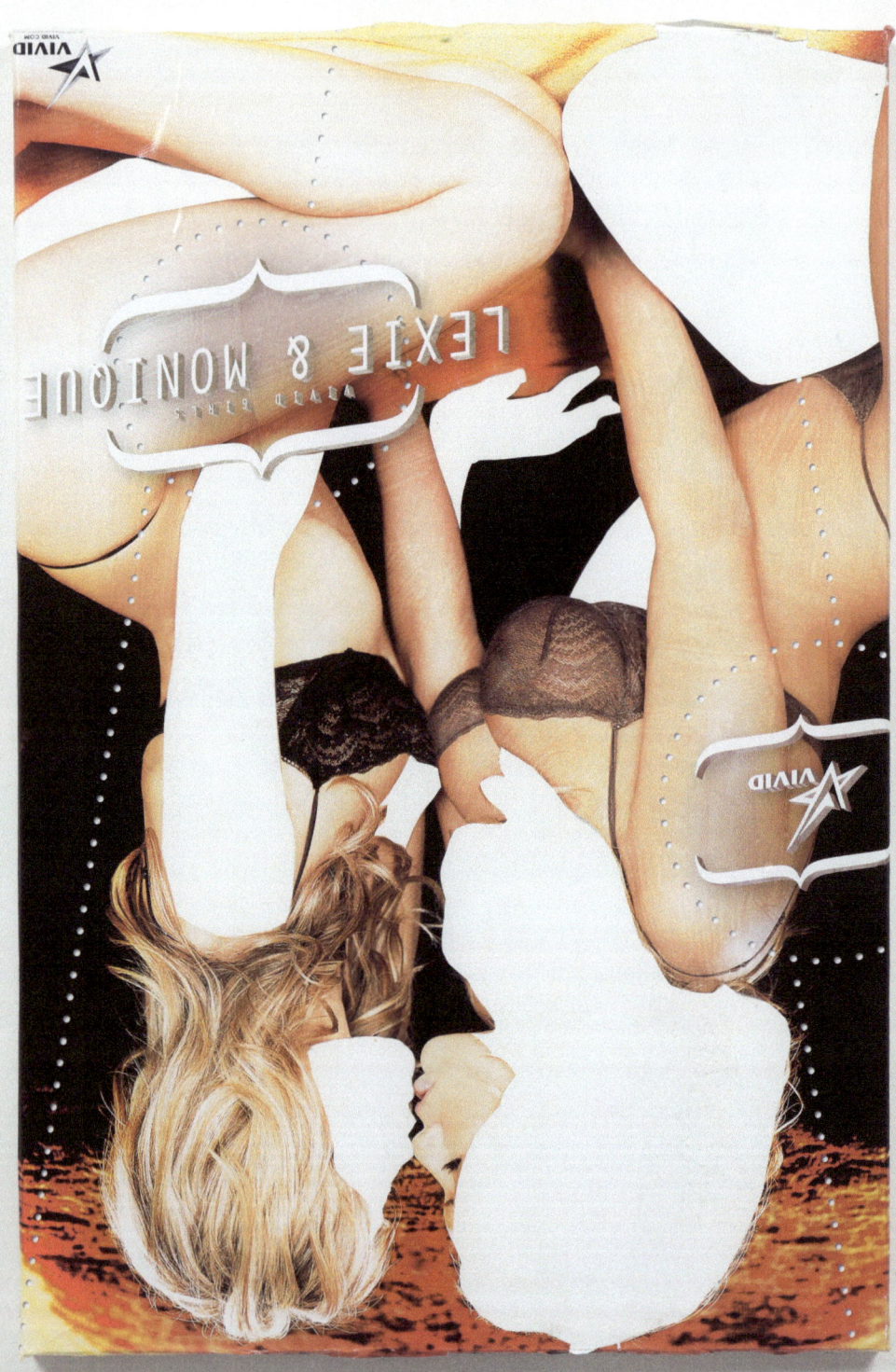

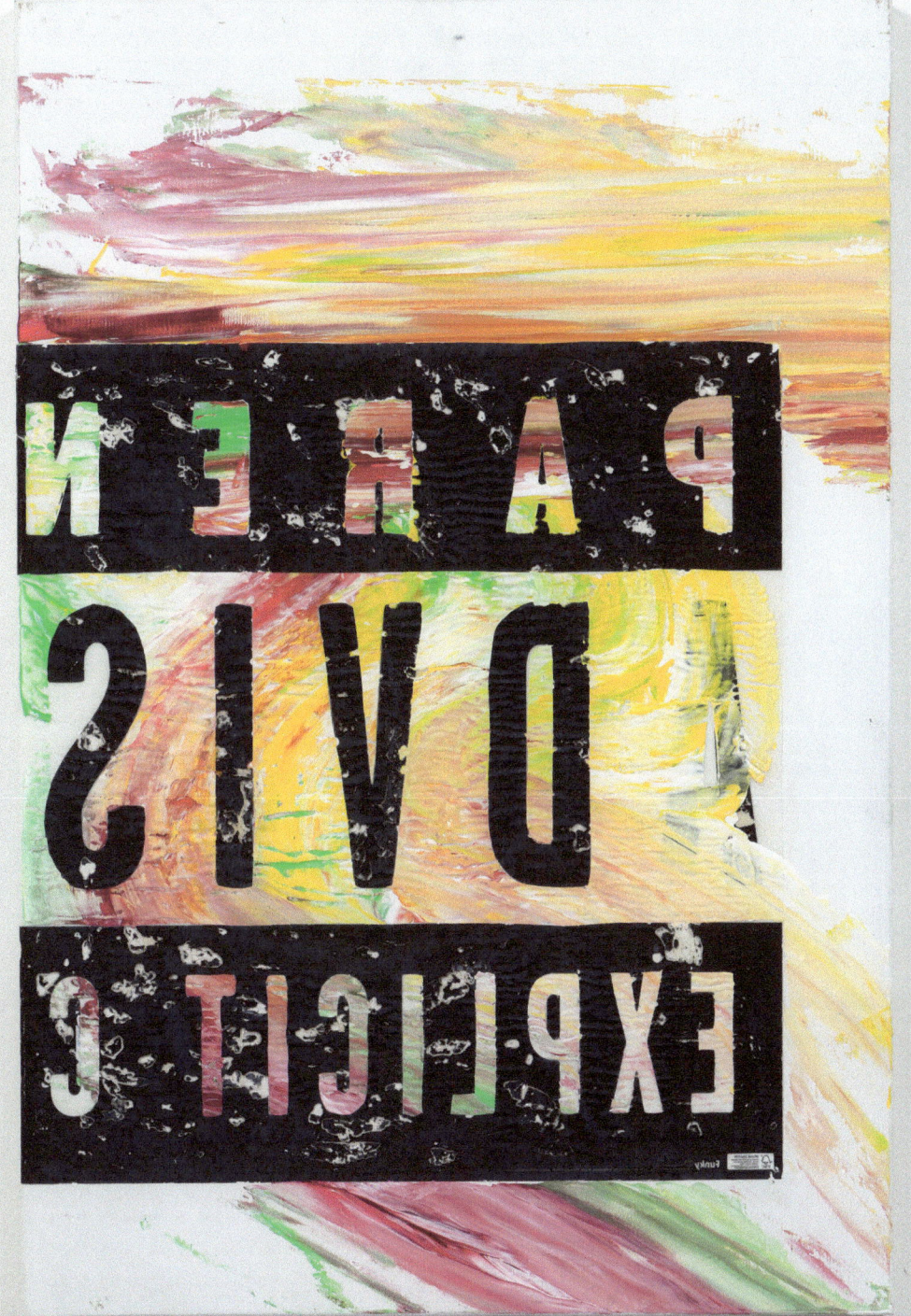

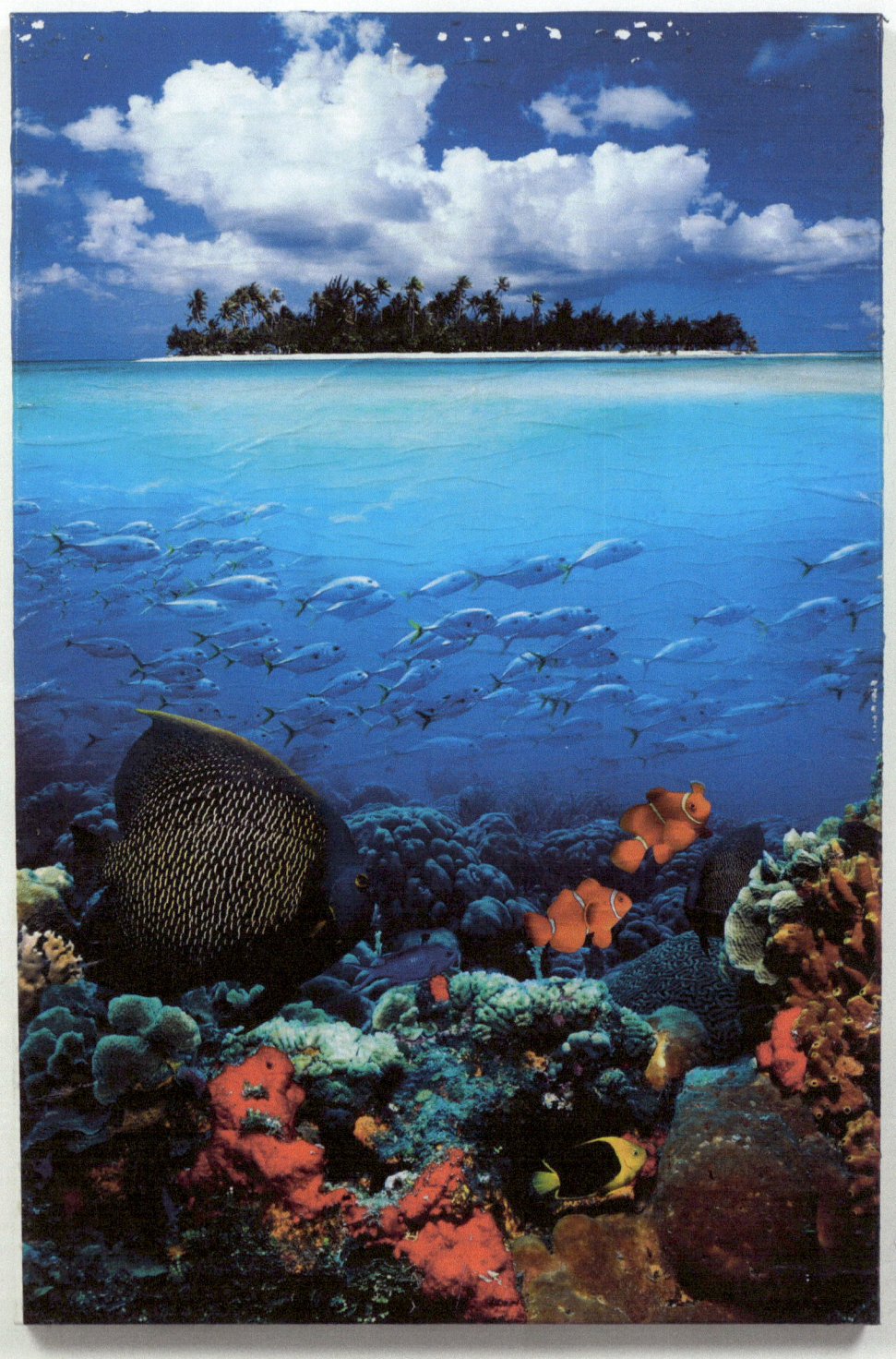

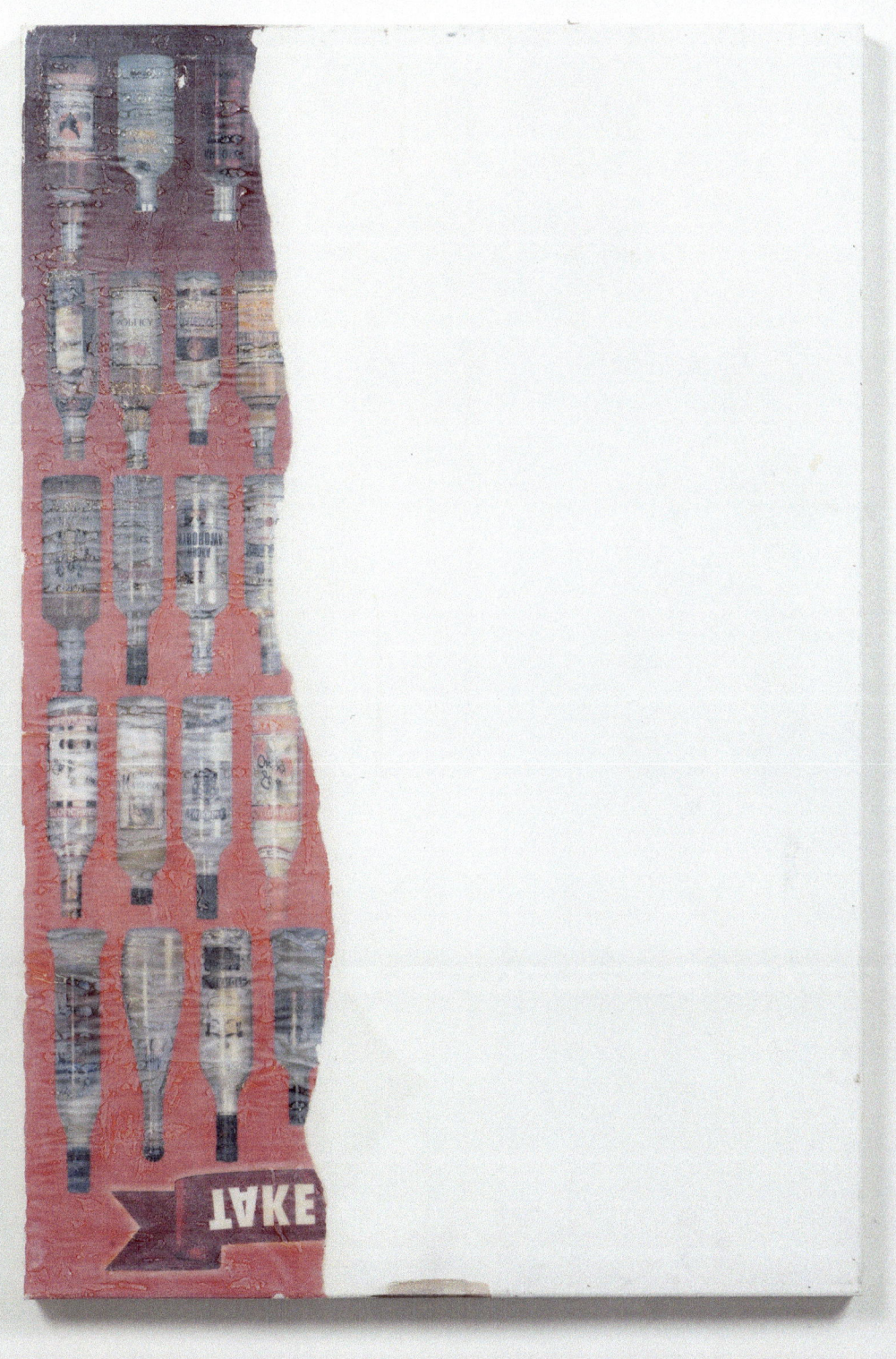

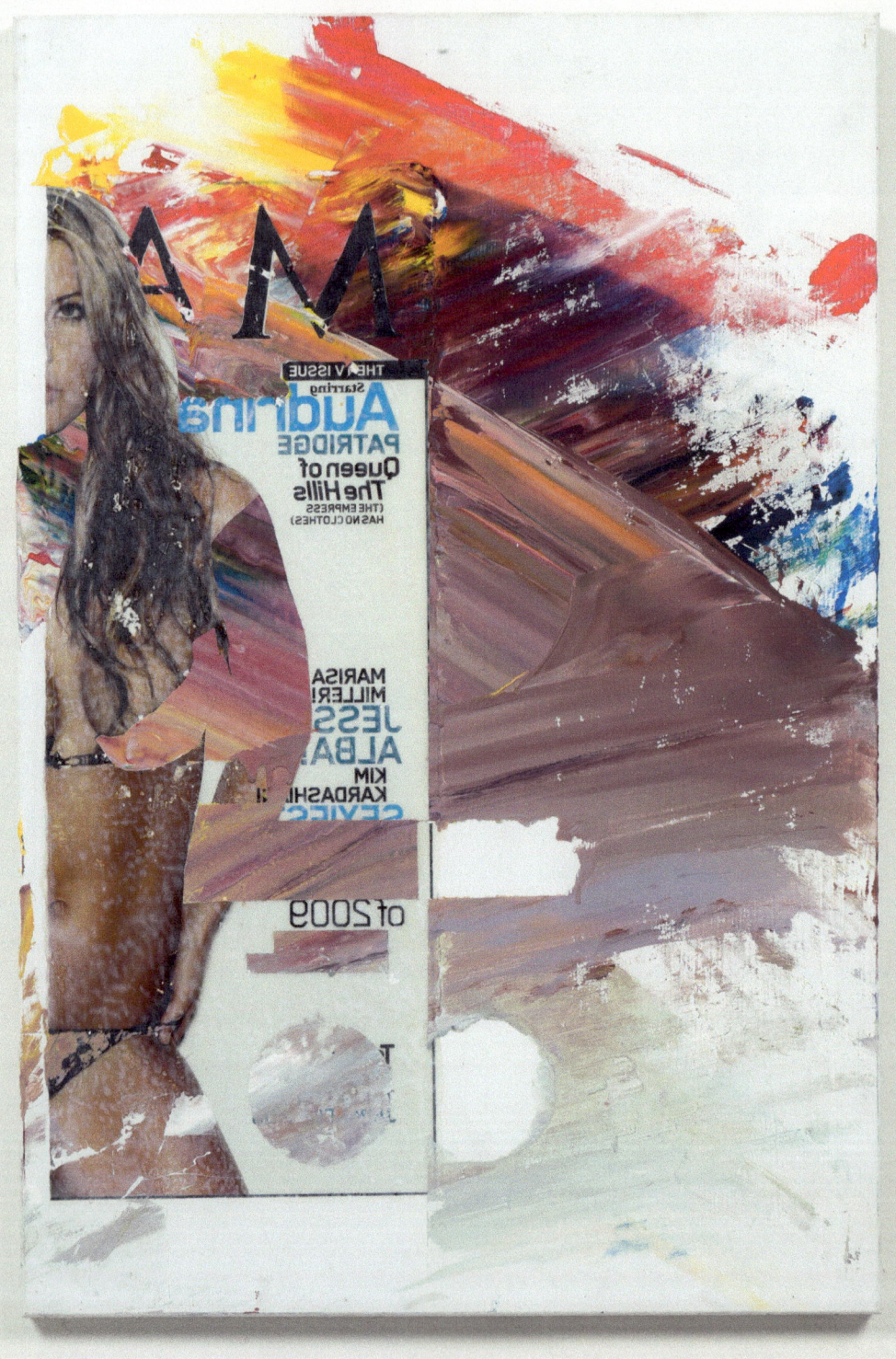

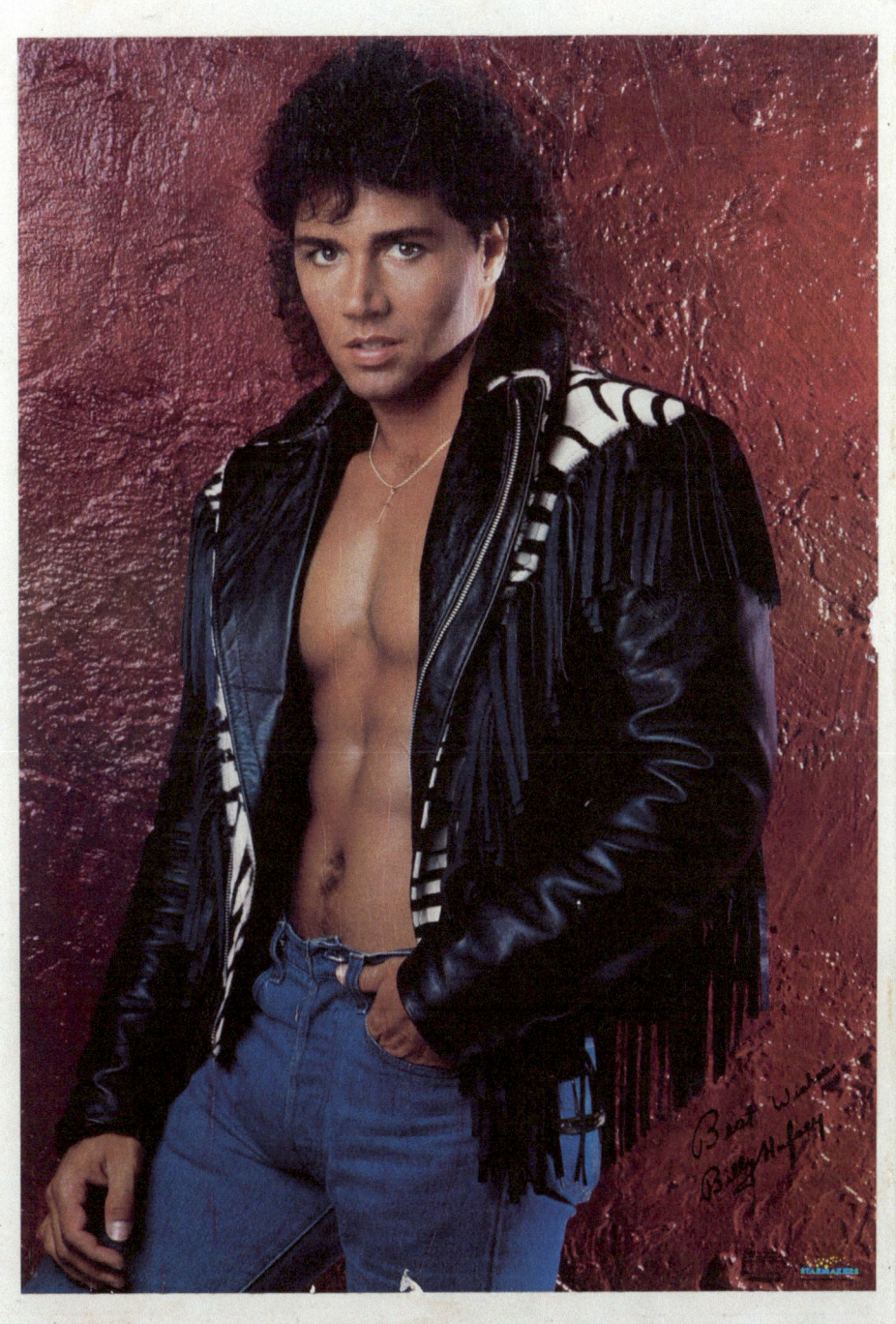

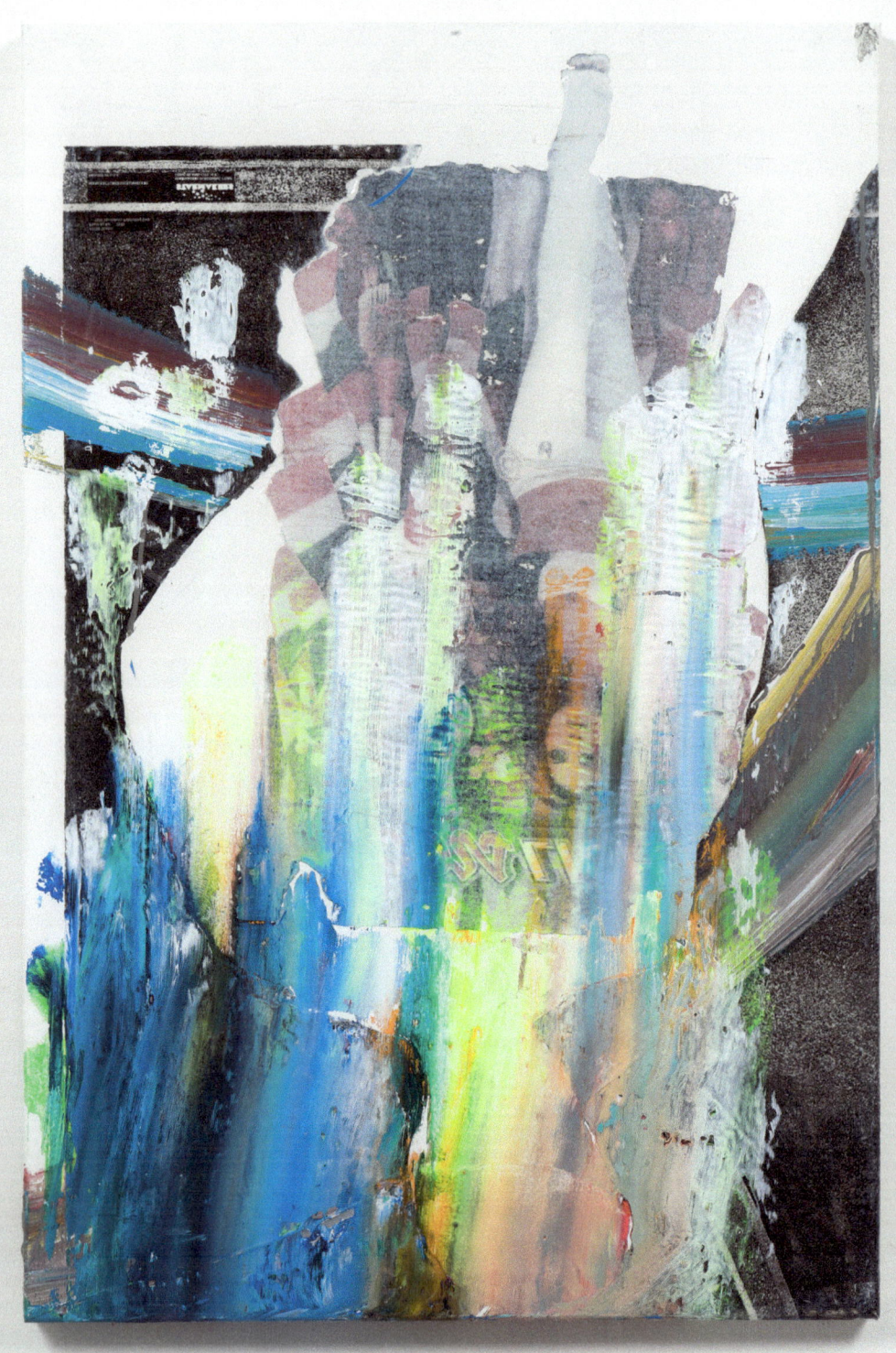

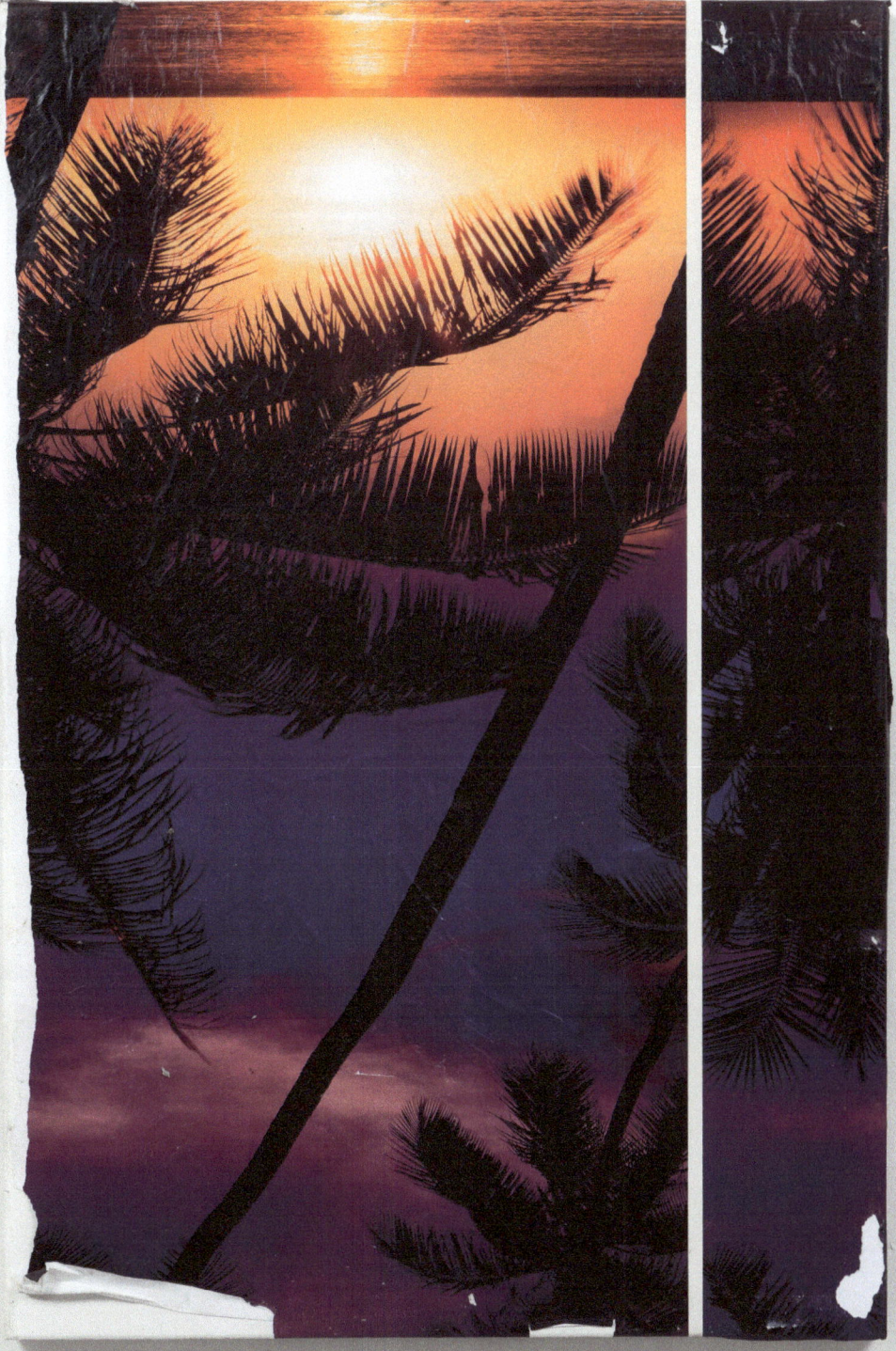

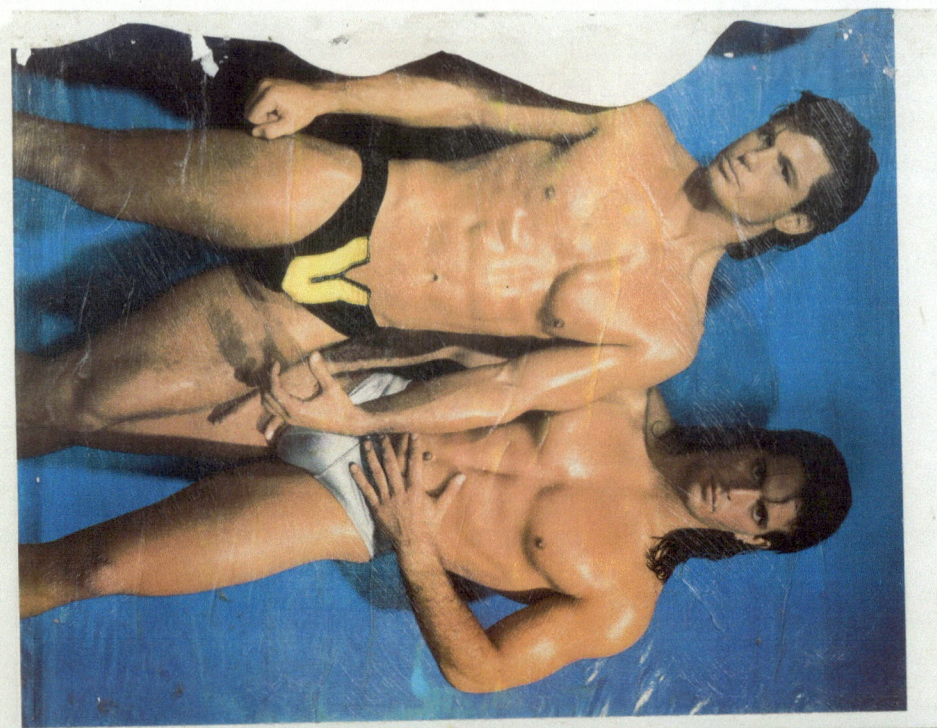

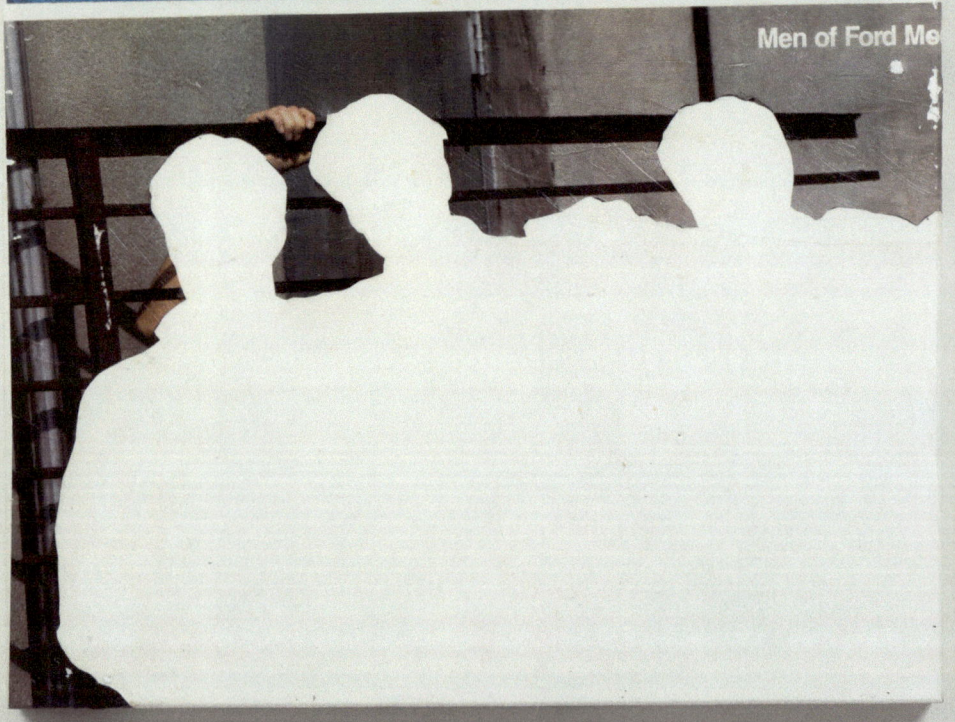

Men of Ford Me

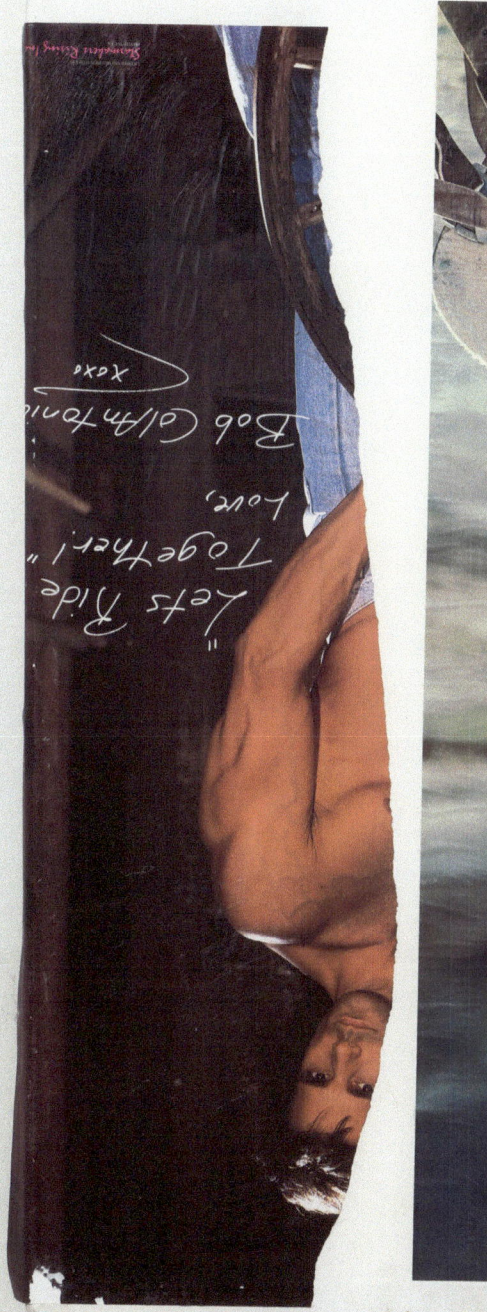

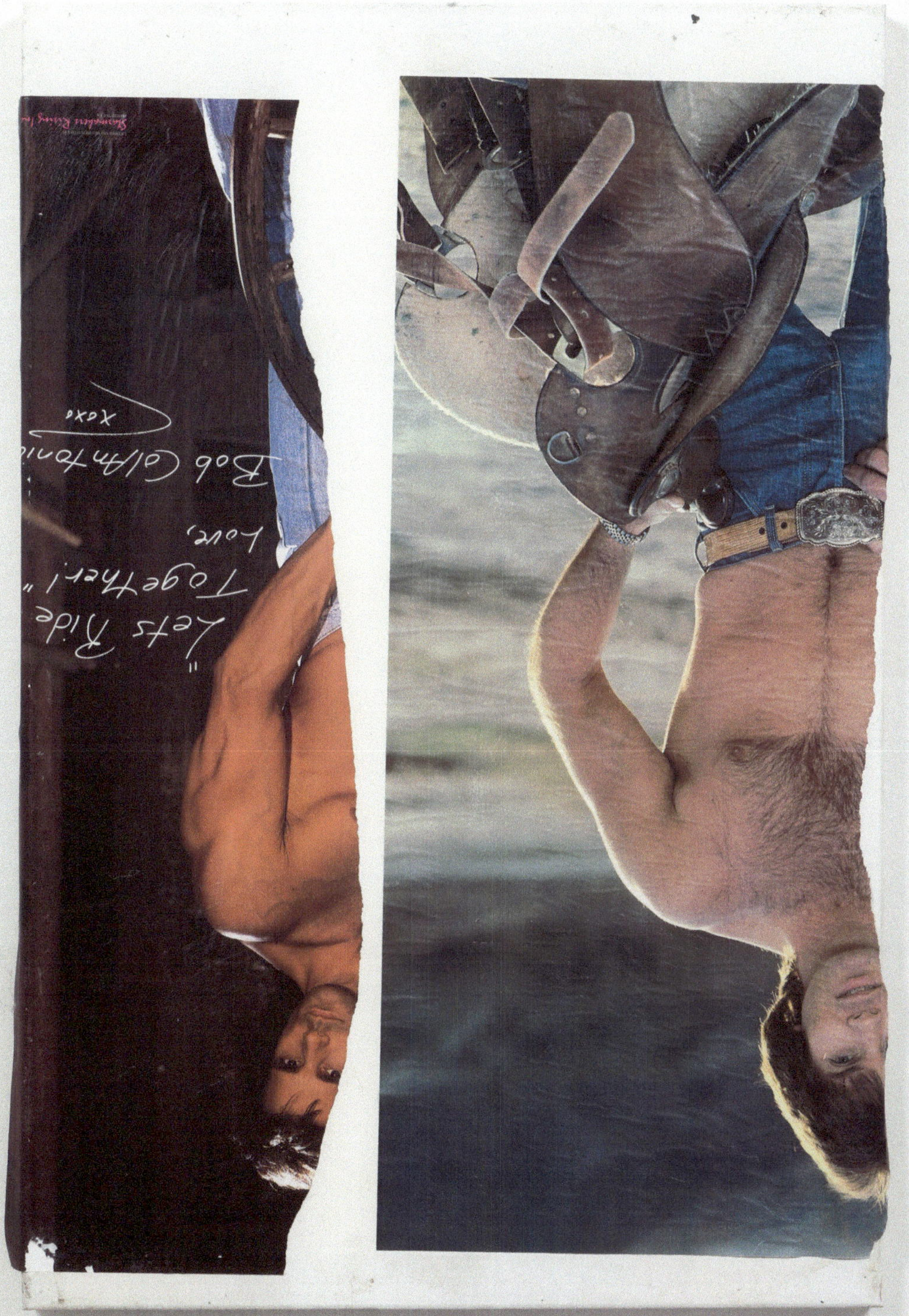

"Let's Ride
Together!"

Love,
Bob California
xoxo

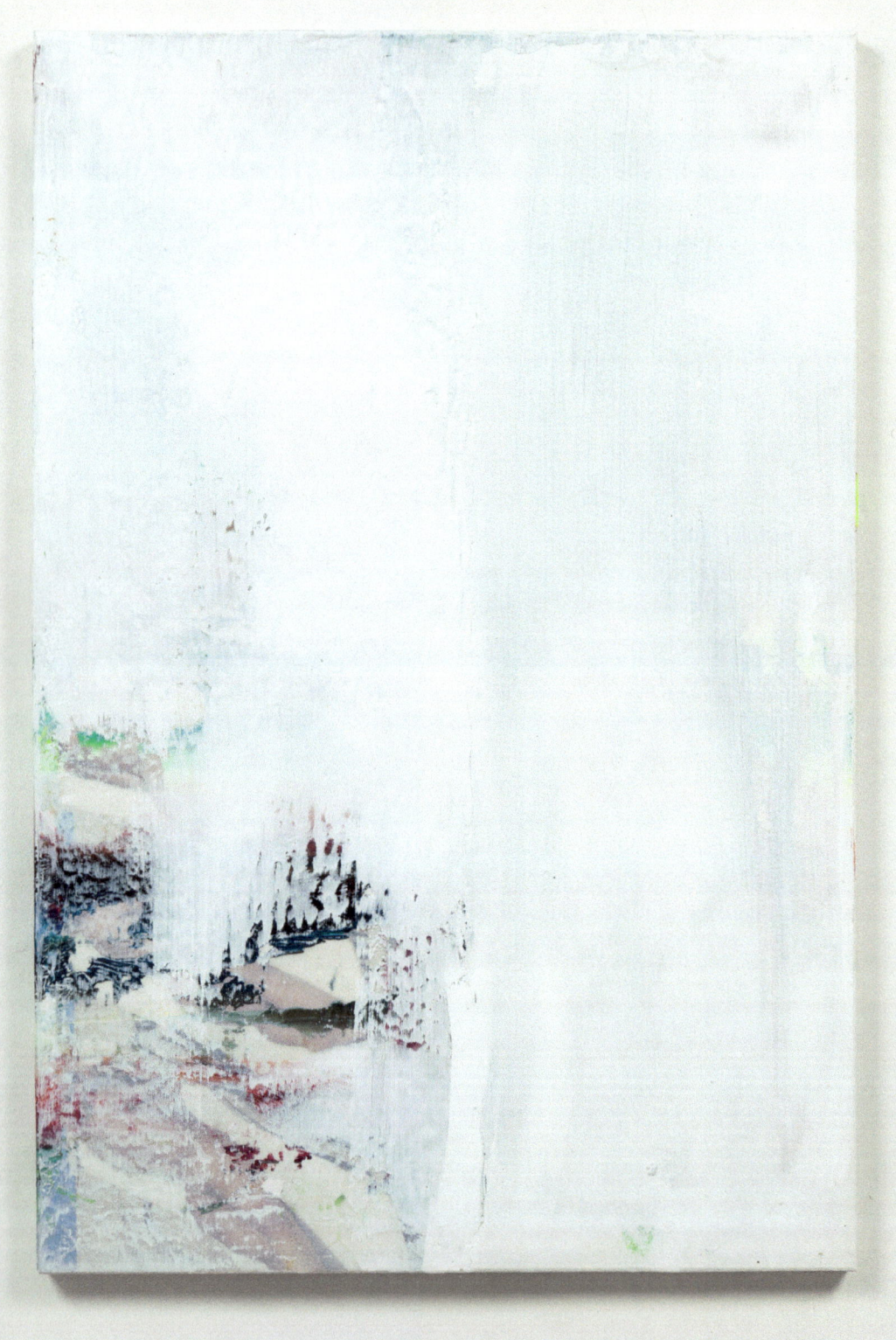

525-525-4547